D0850880

is Going
Within

Mrs D is Going Within

LOTTA DANN

ALLEN&UNWIN
SYDNEY · MELBOURNE · AUCKLAND · LONDON

First published in 2017

Copyright © Lotta Dann 2017

The Mindfulness Revolution, edited by Barry Boyce and the editors of the Shambhala Sun, copyright © 2011 Barry Boyce. All quotes reprinted by arrangement with The Permissions Company, Inc., on behalf of Shambhala Publications Inc., Boulder, Colorado, shambhala. com; 'Here, Now, Aware,' from *A Heart Full of Peace*, copyright © 2007 Joseph Goldstein. All quotes reprinted by arrangement with Wisdom Publications, Inc., wisdompubs. org; *10% Happier* by Dan Harris, copyright © 2014 Daniel Benjamin Harris. All quotes reprinted by permission of HarperCollins Publishers; All Dr Libby quotes reprinted by permission of Dr Libby Pty Ltd; *Mindsight: Change your brain and your life* by Daniel J. Siegel, copyright © 2010 Mind Your Brain, Inc. All quotes reprinted by permission of Scribe Publications; The Mindfulness Summit. All quotes are printed with permission. themindfulnesssummit.com; *Sane New World* by Ruby Wax, copyright © Waxworks Ltd 2013. All quotes reprinted by permission of Hodder and Stoughton Limited; *Mindfulness: An eight-week plan for finding peace in a frantic world* by Mark Williams and Danny Penman, copyright © 2011 Professor Mark Williams and Dr Danny Penman. All quotes reprinted by permission of Rodale, Inc.

Every effort has been made to obtain permission to use copyrighted material in this book.

All rights reserved. No part of this book may be reproduced or transmitted in any form or by any means, electronic or mechanical, including photocopying, recording or by any information storage and retrieval system, without prior permission in writing from the publisher.

Allen & Unwin
Level 3, 228 Queen Street
Auckland 1010, New Zealand
Phone: (64 9) 377 3800

Email: info@allenandunwin.com
Web: www.allenandunwin.co.nz

83 Alexander Street
Crows Nest NSW 2065, Australia
Phone: (61 2) 8425 0100

A catalogue record for this book is available
from the National Library of New Zealand

ISBN 978 1 877505 86 7

Internal design by Anna Egan-Reid
Set in 10.7/18 pt Capita Light
Printed and bound in Australia by Griffin Press

10 9 8 7 6 5 4 3 2 1

MIX
Paper from
responsible sources
FSC® C009448

The paper in this book is FSC® certified.
FSC® promotes environmentally responsible,
socially beneficial and economically viable
management of the world's forests.

For Stanley

Introduction

I am an alcoholic. An A-grade, first-class boozer. I could couch myself in more delicate terms maybe, and call myself a wine-lover or an enthusiastic drinker, but I prefer the more blunt and honest approach. Alcoholic, that's what I am.

The truth is that for almost all of my adult life alcohol has been my constant companion. I drank determinedly and heavily—religiously, almost—from the age of fifteen to the age of thirty-nine. When I first tried alcohol as a fresh-faced teenager, I overdid it and ended up vomiting the entire contents of my stomach into the bath (sickly-sweet bubbly wine and marshmallows, to be precise—an image that has never left me), but that didn't put me off. No way! I was hooked from the get-go, completely drawn to the fun, danger and allure of this magical drug.

I loved the way it felt in my body, trickling up my spine and entering my brain. I loved the way it loosened my limbs and loosened my mood. I loved that it shifted reality, made everything more gnarly and more fun. Teenage me—a heady mix of nerves and rebellion—thought that this wonderful, powerful liquid was the golden ticket to life. And, since I lived in a society where drinking regularly was not only the norm but a celebrated and even encouraged thing to do, it was easy for my teenage crush to steadily morph into an adult love affair. Regularly drinking was how I rolled, and as far as I was concerned imbibing alcohol almost every single day was a very ordinary, grown-up and acceptable thing to do. Five o'clock is wine o'clock right? It certainly was in my world.

I drank through my student years and my early jobs in journalism. I drank as I travelled the country and the world. I drank when I was achieving great things; I drank when I was idle and miserable. I drank in stressful jobs; I drank when unemployed. I drank alone and in groups. I drank when I was single, throughout happy romances, and during dysfunctional relationships.

I used booze to bond with friends, to fit in to groups, to prove that I was a good hostess, and to make myself comfortable in social situations. I drank it to mark achievements, drown sorrows, cure boredom and dull sadness. I drank when celebrating, congratulating, relaxing and memorialising, and when grieving, stressing, being let down or heartbroken. I drank in bars, at work, on aeroplanes, in parks, at the beach, up mountains and sitting on the sofa. I even drank in bed. The only time I *didn't* drink was when I was pregnant or laid up with a tummy bug (sad but true).

Alcohol was just there for me all the time, impacting every experience I had—sometimes elevating my experiences, sometimes smoothing them out, sometimes ruining them. (I have a bunch of best-forgotten memories from events where I got completely blotto and lost the plot—not pretty.)

I can't even begin to imagine how many litres of alcohol I have consumed in my life. I shudder to think about how much booze my internal organs have been forced to process. Beer, wine, gin, whiskey, peach schnapps . . . You name it, I have drunk plenty of it. Mostly though, and certainly towards the end, it was pretty much only wine. Glass after glass after glass of wine. Wine was my constant companion, my trusted friend, my go-to solution, my crutch.

Until it wasn't.

Towards the end of my drinking days I completely lost the ability to moderate my intake. I struggled to have any alcohol-free nights. Once I started drinking I wouldn't stop until all the alcohol in the house was gone. I needed more and more to feel 'full'. Where one bottle of wine in a sitting used to be enough, soon I needed one bottle *plus* another glass (or four).

Time and time again I made promises to myself that I failed to keep—promises like, 'I'm only having one tonight.' I was frequently sloppy, slurry and messy. I'd stumble and fall. There was vomiting.

I was permanently exhausted, hungover and wracked with guilt. Every day was an endless cycle of regretting drinking, recovering from drinking, convincing myself I didn't have a drinking problem, planning on drinking, acquiring alcohol and drinking again. Once it hit my system, I was a goner and I just wanted more, more, more. I was a slave to the drug of alcohol, locked in a miserable binge-and-regret cycle. What had started out as a fun, edgy habit ended up in a dark and dysfunctional place where I had very little pride, strength or self-respect left.

I quit drinking on 6 September 2011 after a particularly miserable Monday-night binge at home, during which I hid an empty bottle of wine from my husband to conceal how much I'd had while he'd been out. This was something I'd never done before. It wasn't so much the events of that evening which forced my point of change, although the dysfunctional behaviour of hiding the bottle was a horrifying new development. Rather, it was the accumulated knowledge gained over the preceding months, during which I'd been trying desperately to gain control of my habit. I *couldn't* gain control, and it all finally came to a head on the night that I hid that empty bottle.

I woke at 3 am that morning full of despair and guilt and

frustration and desperation. This was my personal rock bottom, me at my lowest ebb, a miserable, teary mess. Finally, I accepted that the only way I was going to gain any control was by removing alcohol from my life completely. So I quit, thinking that if I just broke my nasty little drinking habit and learned how to live alcohol-free then life would carry on the same as before.

Boy, was I wrong.

First of all, breaking my 'nasty little habit' was bloody hard work. My brain freaked out when it realised I'd taken away its beloved fix. 'I WANT MY WINE!' it would scream as 5 pm approached. Every. Single. Day. And every single day I'd have to grit my teeth and resist the urge to drink. It was hell. I'd snap and be grumpy with my family. I'd guzzle sugary drinks. I'd clean the house like a mad woman to distract myself. (Never has my house been as clean as it was when I first quit drinking.) I'd force my thoughts forward through the evening, visualising myself getting into bed sober then waking up in the morning without a hangover. I knew that if I could get through the dreaded 'witching hours' of 4 pm to 7 pm without drinking I'd be so happy and proud of myself. Sometimes I'd go to bed at six-thirty just to get the day over with.

Slowly, as the days and weeks passed, the intense physical cravings lessened, and I was able to relax a little.

But beating the cravings was just the beginning.

Next, I had to work on entirely reshaping my identity. No longer was I 'fun Lotta', the upbeat party girl who was always game for a laugh. No longer was I 'cruisy Lotta', the awesome hostess who always had wine on ice to offer her guests. No longer was I 'naughty Lotta', with the twinkle in her eye, getting amongst it into the wee small hours. So who was I instead? My biggest fear was that I would become 'Lotta the boring, sober loser'.

In my early days of sobriety, I struggled through social events, feeling terribly awkward and uncomfortable in my own skin, but—as with everything in sobriety—slowly things took a turn for the better. I discovered that not only did no one care whether I drank or not, but not everyone else was getting hammered all the time. Who knew?! I'd been so locked in to my own boozy mindset that I hadn't noticed how many people take it extremely easy. Furthermore, as I started hanging out without a glass in my hand, I began to realise that—surprise, surprise—alcohol is not the magical, golden ticket to fun I once thought it was.

My entire life, I had given alcohol the power to make events successful, but when I removed it I began to learn that a fun party is a fun party not because my glass contains a brain-bending liquid, but because it's full of elements that make it fun for me—things like a crowd of people I love, a great location, a good atmosphere, music I dig, and me in a good mood and happy in my outfit. I also realised that no amount of booze can improve a boring or nerve-wracking party—all booze does is make you drunk at a boring or nerve-wracking party.

In fact, the longer I went without drinking, the more I started to understand that *all* of my hardwired beliefs and romantic notions about alcohol were complete and utter bullshit. This revelation was HUGE for me and, quite honestly, fascinating.

Here I was at the age of 39, having spent over twenty years worshipping at the altar of my idol, alcohol, and only now was I discovering that it wasn't actually the glorified substance I thought it was. My false god fell off its pedestal, and I started to see it for what it really was: expensive, destructive, foul-tasting shit that did nothing to enhance my life and everything to dull it. I discovered that alcohol wasn't essential for good times; good times are good because they contain naturally enjoyable elements. I discovered that it wasn't the best thing to help me relax at the end of a busy day; relaxing is about being finished with work, putting on comfy pants, lighting a scented candle, connecting with family or unwinding with enjoyable activities. And the biggest mind-shift of all? That alcohol wasn't a 'treat' to 'reward' myself with, but a costly drug that stifled my inner spark and messed me up.

As I slowly clocked up the sober days, and as each of these revelations emerged, I started to feel so great about being free of the stuff. I also started sleeping better, looking better, listening better, concentrating better, parenting better, writing better, singing better, dressing better ... Just being a much better version of myself than I had been before. Fantastic!

Initially, I thought that I'd escaped my drinking days largely unscathed and was on the path to a settled and happy second half of my life—particularly because my story lacks the usual litany of dramatic incidents and monumental cock-ups that can follow in the wake of an alcoholic. But I soon realised this was not the case. I may not have had a criminal record or any failing organs to my name, but did I have widespread emotional deficiencies as a result of my long-term alcohol abuse? Yes indeed.

From the moment I put down the bottle, I was all over the show with my moods. Without a daily liquid suppressant, every tricky emotion burst out of me with overwhelming intensity. I felt raw, drained, teary, super sensitive, uncomfortable, alarmed and confused—sometimes all within the same hour! It was like I'd crawled out of a dark cave—one in which I drank alcohol all the time and never matured properly—and into the bright sunlight. I started to see that alcohol had been a great leveller for me, one that I had used to keep myself on an even keel so that no big highs or lows ever came my way. My regular alcohol habit had dulled all of my feelings and emotions into a fuzzy, boozy mess. I wasn't expecting it, but boy was the shift to living sober a dramatic one. Without my beloved smooth-all, I started living on high alert, feeling every emotion very acutely.

My anger was *rage*. (Ask my sister about the time I punched the wall in the midst of an argument.) My sadness was *despair*. (Ask my friend about the time I sobbed all over her about something that had happened twenty years prior.) These extreme emotional outbursts were deeply uncomfortable. I hated being angry, and I thought that sadness was the worst thing in the world, a feeling to be avoided at all costs. Now that I was sober, these emotions were not only unavoidable, but it also quickly became apparent that I was woefully ill-equipped to deal with them. I couldn't be like, 'I'm having a bad day so I need to do X, Y, Z to look after myself,' or, 'I'm fuming—I need to X, Y, Z to manage this.' I didn't have an X, Y, Z! I had no emotional coping mechanisms, no tried-and-tested methods of dealing with stuff. The only tried-and-tested method I had was to be found in a bottle.

Time has helped somewhat. As I've pushed on through over three years of being sober, I've naturally calmed down and the dramatic lurching from one emotional state to another has quietened. I'm still way more heightened than I was when boozing, but I'm no longer all over the show like when I first quit. I'm much more accepting of my emotions nowadays and am a little more in tune with them coming and going. I'm simply more used to *feeling*. I still don't like tricky emotions, but have grown to tolerate them, much as you would an annoying neighbour or insect bites.

But I still need to do some serious work. The truth is, I've never sat with myself 'in the raw' for long enough to gain any real insight into how I function as a human being. Emotionally, I am very unformed and unresolved. Sure, I've lived a full life and have built up a decent amount of experience and wisdom just from having been on the planet for many years, but having booze as my constant companion in life has prevented me from properly developing any robust coping strategies. I thought I was quite a well-adjusted, mature and wise woman, but putting down the bottle has proved otherwise. I now know that using alcohol for most of my adult life to enhance, distract, avoid, numb and blur reality has messed with my brain chemistry and left me an emotional fledgling.

In many ways, I am writing this book as a typical woman in her forties. My body is that of a typical middle-aged woman (saggy but also soft and strong). My life is full of the typical trappings of middle age (family, mortgage, reading glasses, tea-cup collection). I've experienced many things and have a bunch of memories to show for it. But I lack something important. I lack a solid perspective on myself—how I work, how I process and deal with things. I lack any fundamental knowledge or good tools to help me navigate the remaining years of my life. I'm sober and that is fantastic, but putting down the drink was just the first step. Now I need some next-level help to get me through.

As it stands, I have only two tools in my toolbox that have helped me get to this point in my sobriety. The first tool is massively powerful and the most important, and that is my awesome online recovery community. Thanks to my blog, *Mrs D Is Going Without*, which I started when I first quit drinking, and now Living Sober, the government-funded recovery website I run, I'm constantly surrounded by a wonderful tribe of like-minded people who know exactly what I'm going through. Through my blog, Living Sober and my Facebook, Instagram and Twitter accounts, I'm in daily contact with thousands of equally brave and amazing people who are also working hard to reshape their lives and get sober. We all share openly and honestly about what we're going through, our trials and triumphs, and how we are navigating our sober lives in a world awash with booze. The connections I have made online are incredibly strong and heartfelt. Knowing I can always find a wise and sympathetic ear online when the going gets rough is gold.

The second tool that I have whole-heartedly embraced is the concept of 'sober treats'. All the money that I used to spend on wine, I now spend on special things to treat myself with when I'm feeling low—fresh flowers, scented candles, fancy soaps, delicious chocolates and glossy magazines. These items may sound trite or superficial, but with every purchase I send myself a little self-care message that I am worth being treated well and that I am brave and amazing for quitting booze. It's an important message.

So my toolbox isn't empty. It's just a bit light. At the moment, I don't even have any regular exercise in there, and everyone knows that is super important.

MY TOOLBOX

Recovery community

Sober treats

I need more tools, a better range of tools, deeper tools, more robust tools, because the problem is, life keeps coming at me. Tricky stuff keeps happening—big stuff, hurtful stuff, complicated stuff, painful stuff, confusing stuff—and my tools aren't proving tough enough. I need more techniques for when I'm struggling. My online community is fabulous, but I don't share everything with them (some things are just too private), and a scented candle only goes so far. I'm lucky to have an extremely supportive husband in Corin, a great family and some wonderful friends, but I still desperately feel the need to develop some better coping strategies.

Because, honestly, things aren't going great. Lately I've been experiencing low-grade anxiety, and the sober treats that fall into the 'sweet' category are getting way out of hand—so much so that I'm often caught in a cravings–binge–self-loathing cycle with sugar that is scarily reminiscent of my drinking days.

Sober me needs some serious work. And I've got to do it now, or maybe I will end up back in a bottle, once again using wine as my main emotional coping mechanism.

And that would be extremely dumb.

Chapter 1

What the bloody hell is the problem?

It's 5 pm on a Tuesday. In an hour I need to take my middle son to his Cubs meeting, but before that we'll have dinner. I've got sausages in the frying-pan, potatoes roasting in the oven, broccoli and carrots chopped and ready to cook. My three boys are happily playing video games (or watching YouTube videos of other people playing video games, which is apparently a fun thing to do). While it's quiet, I'm tidying up the house, repositioning things so that they are in their rightful place—something I seem to do endlessly. Corin will be arriving home from his job as TVNZ's political correspondent later. It's an ordinary Tuesday evening. So why do I feel nervy and on edge, like something is wrong?

I can feel it in my belly—there are butterflies there. I mentally run through a list of things that might explain why I am feeling this way. ('There always has to be a clear reason for any emotion,' is how I think.) Butterflies usually equal nerves. Am I nervous about something? Have I got a scary work meeting coming up or a talk to do? Did I just receive a snippy email or nasty text message that I've forgotten about? I stop my tidying and lean over to place both hands on the corner of the kitchen table. I try to reach back into my mind. Nope, can't remember anything specific. So *what* is going on? Is my health worrying me? Is there a social event looming that I'm dreading? *Nothing.* Well, what the bloody hell is the problem, then? Why the butterflies? I can feel them dancing around in my belly and hate that I can't pinpoint why they're there. What on earth are they trying to tell me?

I despise this sense of impending doom, this feeling like I've got something to worry about. It's not an unfamiliar sensation and often—like right now—I can't put my finger on what that something is. I take a deep breath and push myself off the table then carry on tidying things away. As I head back over to the kitchen bench—picking up some shoes on the way and chucking them in the basket—I'm still edgy and worrying about what's wrong. *Surely* there must be a simple and clear answer to why I'm feeling wound up. Did I sleep badly last night? Am I due for my period? Have my food choices been crap lately and that's what's bringing my mood down? No silver bullet springs to mind to explain why I have this nervous tummy. It's annoying.

I keep ruminating on what's wrong as I chuck a couple of glasses into the dishwasher then turn on the elements under various pots and pans. The edginess stays with me as I move about the kitchen, getting dinner plates out of the pantry and putting them on the bench. I need a solution.

It's a pretty fraught conversation, this one I'm having in my head

The only solution I have is to distract myself. I'm very good at this. I reach into the 'secret' cupboard (the one that everyone knows about), where treats for lunchboxes are stashed, to grab two mini bags of salty chips and tear them open. I've been sober for so long that wine isn't on my radar any more and, thankfully, I'm not having a fierce internal debate about whether to have a glass (or five) of merlot to smooth out the edginess… but the chips are a nice, salty distraction for sure.

My phone dings (more distractions—yay!) so I grab it to check out what has arrived. (Must check notifications on my phone immediately or the device will explode.) It's an email from a North American rehab wanting me to publish their infographic about addiction on my blog. Do I want to do that? It apparently details the struggles a child faces when their parent is an addict. Still holding my phone, I grab a tea towel and open the oven door then give the roasting spuds a good shake. They look ready so I turn the oven off and leave the door ajar, then quickly reach into the cupboard for another mini bag of chips. I gobble them down while thinking about emails and infographics and addicted parents and my work in general.

I decide to quickly check Instagram (a couple of new followers, someone's salad, a dog on a beach), then Twitter (two likes on my last tweet, endless boring tips on how to live well, local politicos bickering), then my Facebook page (a couple of new comments, someone has shared a mocktail recipe), and finally my blog to see if there are any new comments (a reader has shared a quote attributed to Helen Keller about the world being full of suffering but also the overcoming of it). I then head to the Living Sober website and navigate to the community section to make sure all the members are playing nice (they are—they're all rallying kindly around someone who relapsed last night, and yet again I'm heartened by how kind and non-judgemental the community is).

When I finally tear myself away from my online world I look over and realise I've overcooked the broccoli. Shit! I drop my phone on the bench and grab the pot off the stove, yelling 'Dinner!' at the boys. The butterflies in my tummy come back into focus and I'm aware my shoulders are tense. I'm definitely on edge. I think about the member who relapsed—it's a bummer, as she'd been doing so well—and mull over the Helen Keller quote, before mentally starting to write an email response to the American rehab. I'm going to have to turn down their request because infographics aren't my thing. I'm busy trying to word my response so that I don't sound uncaring or flippant. I wonder what other bloggers say when they turn down such offers.

There's no sign of my boys.

'Get off your screens now!' I yell, and start worrying once more about this edgy feeling I have. As I drain the hot water off the veggies, I decide it must be my work that has me worried. Not the Living Sober job—that is running very smoothly. It's the media advisory work I'm doing on the side. I'm having trouble managing one relationship in particular, and I'm feeling stressed about the whole situation. I don't know what to do to improve things, and I feel that I'm being totally misunderstood. It's very unsatisfactory. This must be what's got me on edge.

I'm still alone in the kitchen. 'Dinner, now! GET! OFF! YOUR! SCREENS!'

As I begin to plate up, I start a conversation in my mind with the colleague I'm having trouble working with. It's a pretty fraught conversation, this one I'm having in my head, but at least when I'm having it I'm not thinking about the butterflies in my tummy.

Sausages on the plate.

I imagine the colleague being rude and dismissive towards me and I'm being defensive and emotional back.

Broccoli on the plate.

The imaginary conversation is not going well; it's heating up. I'm getting more and more upset.

Carrots on the plate.

'We think your work is shit!'

Potatoes on the plate.

'You don't value what I'm doing!'

'Mum… Mum… Mum… MUM!' I've hardly noticed that the boys have finally arrived in the kitchen.

'What?' I snap at my ten-year-old, then instantly feel bad. The poor guy doesn't realise he's interrupted a tense imaginary work meeting.

'Did you sign the form for the class photo?'

Did I?

'Is there any tomato sauce?' Mr Twelve queries.

Is there?

'Knock-knock!' says Mr Seven.

'Who's there?' I say, handing over the tomato sauce while wondering about class photos and still feeling like I'm locked in an imaginary fight with my colleague. My phone dings again. I grab it. It's a text from Mum, who lives in the South Island: *Call me.*

It's always a sure sign I'm in a gritty phase when I'm eating bagels covered with butter and jam

Mum tells me my step-father has terminal lung cancer. *Holy shit.* The news hits like a bomb and I simply don't know what to do with this awful, gut-wrenching sadness. It hurts, this emotional pain. It hurts down deep. Grief is not something I've had a lot of experience with. I'm struggling big time to know what to do with this. Forget about work woes and nervy tummies—this is the really big stuff of life. I feel utterly wretched that this kind and gentle man who has been an unwavering presence in my life for over twenty years is going. I feel deeply for my mother, who is heartbroken at the prospect of losing her best friend and dear mate. I just feel so deeply sad.

I've had people close to me die before but back then my coping mechanism was booze (and lots of it). Obviously, that particular remedy is gone now. So what to do with this pain? I desperately read up about grief, searching for material on the internet that will give me tips on how to deal with it, watching YouTube clips and TED Talks. Mostly, though, I just keep wishing it away. Wishing he wasn't sick. Wishing this wasn't happening to our family, that we weren't preparing for him going. Why does it have to be this way? I really do wish this wasn't happening.

I feel deeply, heartbreakingly, devastatingly sad. I use the tools I do have, talking to my online community (they are very kind) and diving head first into my sober treats. Well, one type of sober treat, in particular: food. Basically I eat as much as is humanly possible. It's like I can't possibly be full enough. I binge on foods full of sugar and fat. It's always a sure sign I'm in a gritty phase when I'm eating bagels covered with butter and jam. Quite why I consider these foods to be treats is beyond me—they might be yummy immediately, but the after-effects are grim. I feel fat and unhealthy and weak.

I have other ways to distract myself from the sadness: cooking, cleaning, working and worrying about tricky colleagues also keep me occupied. My mind has kicked into overdrive, fretting about the less-than-satisfactory relationship I feel I have with that colleague, and the tenuous position I feel I'm in with regards to the work. In real life, nothing new about this situation has developed, but it sure has escalated inside my head. By now, I've spent so many hours carrying out a crazy imaginary feud with my colleague that the argument has dug out well-worn pathways in my mind and I've lost sight of what's real and what's not. It almost feels comforting to keep returning to this fierce dialogue in which I'm battling for my point of view to be heard, and so I do go back to it—again and again and again.

And, more than ever, I busy myself online. Every new Instagram follower, Twitter notification, Facebook like or blog comment is a welcome distraction. So, too, is parenting my three boisterous sons. They're extremely busy, and even more so than normal as we're heading into the end of the school year. There are endless forms to fill in, gifts to be bought, plates of food to be prepared and activities to get to.

But, during the moments in the day when I'm not able to distract myself with sugar, technology or the kids, my mind wanders like buggery and my thoughts are busy and noisy. In the shower, driving the car, washing the dishes, any time when I'm alone and doing something menial, I'm actually miles away, lost in thought, feeling annoyed that my work relationships aren't easier or feeling sad and wishing my step-father wasn't dying. It's exhausting and depressing. It's no bloody fun at all.

Chapter 2

I'm far from a 'happy, joyous, free' housewife, that's for sure

Eight days before Christmas, just a few short weeks after his diagnosis, my step-father dies. We travel to the South Island for the funeral, which is a small gathering in my mother's garden. I wear sunglasses during the service and try to distract myself by thinking about other things (I literally try to get lost in thought, remembering happy times), but it's hard to tune out the poems being read and speeches being made. I cry a lot.

Once the formalities are dealt with, I slip into social mode. There are a few tricky dynamics with some people, which is a little stressful. There is booze flowing, of course, because booze always flows at social events in this country of mine, but I'm not bothered by that. No one is getting sloppy and I have relaxed an awful lot since I first stopped drinking. (Back when I first quit, I used to take every alcoholic drink consumed by another person as a huge slap in the face, but nowadays I feel much more chilled out about having it around. Other people can have it; I'm not interested in the stuff. Booze really has lost its allure for me.) However, that doesn't mean I wouldn't dearly love to escape the deeply uncomfortable sadness that is overcoming me right now—and thankfully there is cake!

After the funeral there's no time to pause and gently recover from the shock and emotional outpourings, as we're straight into Christmas. We launch into the silly season head first, racing around visiting friends and relatives, socialising up a storm. All this interacting and negotiating with other people is tiring, and there are complicated relationships simmering away that I feel hyper-aware of. Why do relatives always have such brilliant button-pushing abilities?

After a couple of weeks of hard-out socialising, Corin, the boys and I go camping for a week. I'm hoping the deck-chair lifestyle will give me a chance to finally de-stress, regroup and unwind, but it doesn't. Pausing all the busyness only serves to highlight how unrelaxed I am. There's still so much noise whirring around in my mind. I'm far from a 'happy, joyous, free' housewife, that's for sure.

I'm also still busy working online. My social media spaces require constant updating and checking for feedback (at least, I choose to constantly check them for feedback), and I'm permanently on duty as moderator at Living Sober. The website is super busy of course, because this time of year is particularly hard for people who are trying to give up booze. (They don't call it the 'silly season' for nothing.) Members are turning to the site in their thousands and leaning on each other for help navigating social events and family tensions. Things hum along smoothly—the community vibe is unfailingly kind and supportive—but then a bunch of bastard spammers set their spam bots on us and we get hit with hundreds of bogus sign-ups and comments. It's a spam attack like I've never experienced before—intense and nasty. It gets so bad, the techies have to take the entire site down for a few days while they fix the problem. I'm having to liaise with them and ease the concerns of worried community members from my 'office' at the campsite (my deck-chair outside the tent). This is not the completely stress-free holiday I might have hoped for.

Distracting myself with bad foods and the internet isn't cutting it any more

I'm tight. Mentally, I'm tight. Emotionally, I'm tight. My shoulders are tight. My breath is tight. There are butterflies in my belly regularly and I'm pretty sure it's a symptom of low-grade anxiety. I constantly try to reassure myself by thinking that all of this is normal—spammers attack, people die, families are complicated, everything is OK. I'm generally in good health. My husband is good. My kids are good. Everything is as it should be. It's OK. Really, it's OK. Yet I remain tight and on edge.

Why do I feel so unsettled? Why is my brain whirring along nineteen to the dozen all the time? Why have butterflies clustered in my belly? Why do I have endless heated discussions with people in my head? Why am I not moving through my days in a blissful state of Zen-like calm? Why am I so goddam tight inside and out?

On top of all this worrying, I also feel slightly fraudulent because of the nature of my work. I'm a recovery advocate; I spend all my time talking online about how great it feels to be sober (and really it does, believe me—I am a million miles from the boozy hell I was living three years earlier), yet I'm hardly the model of a super-calm, fully resolved, perfectly Zen housewife.

In fact, in some ways, the longer I go in sobriety, the harder things seem to get. Not the not-drinking part—that's easy. Like I've said, I no longer crave booze or have the knee-jerk reaction to reach for a substance to blur the edges of my brain. But, while time has removed my urge to drink, it has also made me more aware of my inability to calmly process and deal with all the stuff that keeps going on in my life. It's almost as if the novelty of sobriety has worn off, which is a real bummer. I used to experience lovely waves of happiness and pride every time I ground through tough times without drinking— and those proud feelings would act as a fantastic buffer to the tricky emotions. Just thinking, *Yay, me! I got through that without drinking!* used to be a wonderful antidote to any shitty times, but the longer I'm sober, the more ordinary it becomes and subsequently the less proud of it I remember to feel. Not drinking is a given now; it's the normal way that I live. In many ways, this is fantastic—how great that I have got to this place in my sobriety!—but it's also a bit of a downer because that pride really did help to counterbalance the sharp edges of life.

Much like when I reached the point where I realised I had to stop drinking, I slowly come to the conclusion that something has to change. Distracting myself with bad food and the internet isn't cutting it anymore. I need some new tools in my toolbox, some new techniques. I need a new plan.

But what?

Everybody and their dog (if their dog has a Twitter account) is banging the drum about mindfulness

The internet leads me to the answer. No surprises there, given how much time I spend online and how constantly bombarded I am with other people's ideas and messages. On my various social media accounts I follow hundreds of addiction experts, fitness boffins, health gurus, researchers, authors, rehabs and other organisations devoted to wellness and recovery. They all keep going on about tools and practices that are necessary if you want to maintain a happy lifestyle. Twitter in particular keeps giving me snappy one-liners that until now I've been ignoring. But, given I'm so wound up and struggling with things, I'm finding it hard to ignore the endless wellness chatter.

Take yoga, for example. Yoga is touted everywhere online as the answer to everything—and I mean *everything*.

- #yoga is powerful for helping people with #depression
- #yoga is helpful for improving arthritis pain
- Need to improve your balance? #yoga is the key
- #yoga lowers stress and anxiety
- #yoga can teach us about happiness and contentment
- How #yoga can help clean your house

OK, I made that last one up, but there is a theme here. Yoga is the miracle cure, according to the internet. I'm not convinced.

In fact, I heartily disagree. I'd like to never have to think about yoga again, except it keeps bloody well being tweeted about. Can it really be that good?

Another thing that keeps being mentioned in Twitter's 140-character bursts is 'gratitude'. There's a lot of talk in recovery circles about gratitude and how beneficial it is if practised daily. Sober bloggers often write gratitude posts listing all the good things in their lives. Lots of people in my personal Facebook feed have been doing 'seven days of gratitude' lists, and all the wellness boffins on Twitter are obviously in favour of it.

- The daily practice of gratitude is one of the conduits by which your wealth will come to you #gratitude

- A moment of #gratitude makes a difference in your attitude

- Begin with #gratitude and watch the #miracles flow your way

- Never let the things you want make you forget the things you have #gratitude

- Listing what I am grateful for is a practice that contributes to a sense of joy and peace #gratitude

All right, Twitter. I hear you. Clearly gratitude is a helpful thing, but how do I incorporate it into my life so that it actually makes a difference? I'd love it if I could just write out one list of all the things I am grateful for and then be miraculously filled with joy and peace for evermore. Maybe I'll start now.

I'm grateful that I no longer drink alcohol.

I'm grateful that I have a lovely family.

I'm grateful that I have a nice house to live in.

I'm grateful that I have the internet to connect me to a world of stimulating people who want to help me live better even though I don't always get what they're on about.

I do get that gratitude is something that needs to be practised in an ongoing way for it to have any real benefit, but how on earth do you bring it into your life on a regular basis? I have no idea how to do that.

The big kahuna, though, seems to be mindfulness. This is the thing I find is most often talked about by all sorts of people in all of my internet spaces. I *think* mindfulness might be like meditation but slightly different, but I'm not entirely sure about that. In fact, I really don't know much about mindfulness at all, other than that it gets a lot of air time. Like, a *lot*. It is the hot trend among wellness experts. Everybody and their dog (if their dog has a Twitter account) is banging the drum about mindfulness. They've been going on about it for so long it's virtually impossible to ignore. Problem is, I think it sounds freakish and wishy-washy and not like something I'd be keen on at all.

> Thoughts may be treated like sounds: you hear them, you recognise them, you let them go #mindfulness

Thoughts may be treated like sounds? What the hell does that mean?

> Real but not true: freeing ourselves from harmful beliefs #mindfulness #meditation

Say whaaaaat? How can something be real but not true?

> When practising #mindfulness there is nothing to do, nowhere to go, no to-do list

Huh? So it's nothing at all? What is it then, if it's nothing? How can something be nothing?

> #mindfulness is the aware, balanced acceptance of the present experience. It isn't more complicated than that

Awareness of the present experience? How can life be anything *but* awareness of the present experience? I'm aware of everything I'm doing all the time. At least I think I am. Aren't I overly aware—in fact, isn't that my problem? Is mindfulness just going to make me even more hyper-aware of everything and therefore even more wound up and unsettled? What's the point then?

 In meditation, do not seek anything at all. Simply become comfortable in the void. Become the formless consciousness beyond the mind #mindfulness

What the—? This is bonkers talk. Formless consciousness beyond the mind? And this stuff about meditation, is that what mindfulness is? Is mindfulness actually meditation? Sitting cross-legged with your eyes closed and chanting? That's just for hippies, isn't it? Monks on mountaintops?

Honestly, the thought of meditation terrifies me. I think it sounds boring, introspective, boring, scary, boring, indulgent, hard work, and did I mention boring? And well, frankly, a challenge. How on earth am I going to fit it into my life? I am busy. I run a website that has me online seven days a week. I am also a recovery advocate, blogger, full-time housewife and mother to three boisterous boys. I like watching *Dr. Phil* (he's so wise!), listening to pop music and catching up with girlfriends over coffee or dinner or a movie. I've got no time for mountaintops or chanting.

Part of me just wants to keep ignoring all this waffle about mindfulness, but the other part of me—the part desperately seeking a solution to my fraught state of mind—won't let me. I need something to help soothe my uncomfortable emotions and quieten the butterflies in my tummy.

Maybe this trendy new mindfulness thing is the way to go. Lately even the mainstream media appears to be jumping on the mindfulness bandwagon. Headlines like 'Mindfulness Therapy as Good as Medication for Chronic Depression' and 'Meditation Really Works' stare at me every day from local news websites. And the tweets keep showing up in my feed.

> Mindfulness offers support for working with intense and difficult emotions

Well, that sounds good. So, this thing that is mindfulness is nothing, but something, and could help me deal with emotions? That can't be a bad thing. I need help here, because I'm not coping brilliantly. I really do think my coping mechanisms are weak, to say the least (not that surprising, given I spent most of my adult life using alcohol as my main emotional-management tool). Fingers crossed I'll live to be a ripe old lady, which means I've got decades of sober living ahead of me, and big life stuff is going to keep happening, and my moods are going to keep happening, and I'm always going to be busy because life is bloody busy. I need new tools, and maybe mindfulness is the answer.

> The secret to feeling total relief and inner peace? Embrace everything just as it is. #mindfulness and #meditation for beginners

Well, that sounds like just the ticket. Total relief and inner peace is *exactly* what I'm after. But again, precisely how do I 'embrace everything just as it is'? What does that even mean? I'm doing that already, aren't I? Isn't that just called living? I'm dealing with everything that comes at me—I've no choice but to embrace it. It happens; I deal with it. Isn't that embracing everything just as it is ? Then again, I'm far from inner peace, so maybe I'm not.

All right, Twitterati. You've got me. My interest has been piqued. I'm going to explore these practices that you're all banging on about. This is a firm decision. I'm going to make this my next project. My first big project was getting sober; the next is going to be developing some new wellness strategies and coping mechanisms for dealing better with life. I'm going to learn how to navigate tough situations, people and emotions in robust ways. I'm going to make a concerted effort. I'll sign up for courses, read books, listen to podcasts, make lists. You name it, I'll do it.

I'll learn all these new wellness strategies and they'll solve all my problems. Then, like magic, once I've learned them all I'll be a flexible, grateful, mindful guru and the most Zen housewife you have ever seen. All will be peaceful in my world and in my brain. I'll be a perfect human!

Easy, right?

Chapter 3

'To be honest, I've been worried lately that you're getting depressed'

I inform Corin of my decision over dinner the next evening. The boys have gobbled down their food in record time and left the table, so it's just the two of us now, chewing slowly like cows (or that's how we always feel compared to our sons). Corin's just finished telling me about his stressful day at work, which was filled with pressing deadlines, demanding bulletin editors and grumpy politicians, when I say, 'Well, anyway, I've got news. I'm embarking on a new project. I need to get some more tools together to help me deal with stuff. So I'm going to start exploring ... uh ... mindfulness and ... maybe yoga ...

and stuff.' I'm feeling energised and determined, but also a bit embarrassed. I still think mindfulness sounds a little kooky, and Corin knows I have a strong dislike for yoga.

'OK,' he replies, slowly chewing his cud—sorry, lasagne. He sounds interested even though I'm pretty sure he'd never explore such things himself. 'I think it'll be good for you to have something new to put your energies into.' He reaches for his water and then drops a bombshell. 'To be honest, I've been worried lately that you're getting depressed.'

Holy heck! This comes like a bolt from the blue. I'm so taken aback I don't even know how to react. I've thought of myself as many things lately, but I hadn't gone so far as to consider myself depressed. But Corin is right. I *am* more prone to low states of mind now that I'm sober, and things have been particularly bad lately with my step-dad's death and my work pressures.

'I'm not depressed, I don't think,' I tell him, 'but I'm not great. I'm wound up. Sort of anxious, I suppose. I feel in a bit of a rut in general.'

I feel like a failure admitting this because shouldn't everything be great all the time now that I'm not necking wine like it's going out of fashion? Sadly, this isn't the case. Aside from the obvious sadness and grief I've been dealing with lately, I am struggling a bit more overall with my general emotional state. My anger still comes out pretty strongly at times, I often have anxious butterflies in my tummy, and my shoulders are regularly tight from stress. Sometimes I experience a strange restlessness where I feel 'itchy' and a bit directionless. I used to think it was boredom (and I'd often say that I drank because I was bored), but I don't think this 'boredom' I'm experiencing is actually boredom. I think it's a symptom of something else ... but who knows what. A 'hole' inside me that I need to fill? But how? I tend to fill it nowadays with salty chips or sugary treats, checking my online spaces over and over (and over and over), playing Scrabble online, writing blogs, watching *Keeping Up with the Kardashians* or *The Walking Dead* (so in love with Daryl), or having fierce imaginary discussions with tricky people in my life.

I'm sick of all of it.

I'm sick of going around and around the internet in a directionless manner.

I'm sick of working myself up by getting into fights with people inside my head, when no actual resolution is occurring in real life.

I'm sick of mindlessly pigging out on 'treat' foods that are not actually treating my body well at all.

I'm sick of feeling distracted all the time.

I'm sick of flaring up and bickering with the kids when they are trying to bicker with me.

I'm sick of feeling sad about things that are out of my control, and worried because I know there are many more sad things to come.

I'm sick of arriving places in my car and realising that I don't remember any of the journey because I've been so lost in thought along the way.

I'm sick of it all, and I want something to change.

I do, of course, feel incredibly proud of myself for kicking booze to the curb—but that feeling has lost some of its shine. I'm starting to understand what the famous saying 'Putting down the drink is just the beginning' means. Taking alcohol out of your life is monumental and wonderful—a hugely enriching and positive thing to do—but then the real work begins. Now it's time for me to do some concerted 'next stage' work on myself. I desperately want to become more peaceful inside of myself, deep down in my core. The only thing is that, since I've never done this before, I don't know the first place to start. In the absence of any better ideas, mindfulness (and related 'wellness' strategies) seem my best (and maybe my only) starting point.

Oh, gawd. Just thinking about a life filled with gratitude lists, downward dogs, quiet contemplation and focusing inwards sounds stupid and uncomfortable and boring. I'm deeply sceptical. How can these things possibly improve my day-to-day experience? They're not going to stop loved ones from dying, make Facebook any less alluring, turn my kids into perfect angels, or remove all the tricky people from the world. But, goddammit, something has to change.

It's true. I'm really not in a great space right now—something Corin has just confirmed with his statement about me being depressed. I haven't got any other bright ideas, so these wellness strategies are it. Anyway, I like to have a forward-looking plan. Plans are good. Just having this plan has lifted my mood somewhat.

Corin is right. I need something new to put my energies into. A new project!

It's a bit too McMindfulness

The next day, I'm in town having coffee with a new friend at a hipster cafe. I don't know him that well but he's pretty cool, and it's always nice to meet face-to-face with other people in recovery, as most of my sober friends are online. Sipping my decaf flat white I decide it's safe to share with this like-minded soul a little about how I need to sort my mental shit out. I mention the m-word.

'Oh, mindfulness!' He's instantly down with the vibe—like, what took you so long?!—and starts raving about a meditation app he uses called Headspace.

'Are you actually meditating?' I ask, struggling to picture this young bearded dude taking time out to go inwards, but he nods easily. I'm desperate to pry further and ask, 'What do you do? When do you do it? How does it work? What is it like?' But I don't want to be too pushy, so instead I get my phone out to try to find this app. Sure enough, there it is—in all its orange-and-blue cartoony glory. Headspace: Meditation made simple. I download it and sign up for the free ten-day trial. I don't feel like laying out any dosh just yet.

At home after my coffee date, I log in to Headspace. It's incredibly slick and modern-looking, all pale pastel colours and blobby, colourful cartoon figures juggling and waving and saying, 'Welcome!' I figure the juggling must be a metaphor for busy modern lives—all those figurative balls in the air—rather than because the app is aimed at circus performers.

I click on a link to an animated video called 'How It Works'. It's short—under two minutes long—and very cutesy and slick. Cute cartoons do cute things with cute sound effects while a cute-sounding English man speaks to me about what the app will do for me. He tells me to think of it like a 'gym member-ship for the mind' and that I can learn the basics of meditation by listening to him for just ten minutes a day for ten days in a row. And I can do that for free! Well, that sounds doable. I like free.

I watch some of the other animated videos, and they're all just as cutesy and slick and voiced by the same super-laid-back English guy. I'm not sure the pastel figures and their cute noises are really doing it for me. It's a bit too McMindfulness. I feel babied. And who is this Zen-sounding dude doing all the talking anyway?

I go back to the main menu and see a link called 'Who's Andy?'—who indeed?! When I click on it, up pops a photo of a trendy dude with a youthful, tanned face and smooth bald head, smiling broadly. *This* is Andy, the voice of all things Headspace. Apparently he's a meditation and mindfulness expert, presenter, writer of three bestselling books, and has been featured in numerous magazines and on TV. He's also an ordained Tibetan Buddhist monk *and* a trained circus performer—yes, a circus performer! Is there no end to this man's talents? This could explain the juggling balls.

I decide to listen to Day One of the trial right now. Go, me! This is great. I'm already mentally adding it to my toolbox.

MY TOOLBOX

Recovery community

Sober treats

Mindfulness (Headspace)

Andy tells me to sit comfortably in a chair with my eyes open, then instructs me to shut them gently and start focusing on my breath. I lower my eyelids and immediately feel worried that my posture isn't correct because the sofa I'm sitting on is too low. My bum is lower than my knees. That's bad posture, isn't it? Maybe this isn't the right spot for me to sit and chill.

While I'm shuffling around worrying about my posture and trying to sit more upright, Andy is saying, 'Notice the gentle rising and falling of your chest as you breathe.' I do that for a nanosecond then I start wondering how much this bald ex-monk is going to charge me for a subscription after the free ten-day trial is over. I start thinking about our household budget and whether I can justify spending money on meditation apps, then I start thinking about how much money I used to spend on wine and wonder where the hell all that money is now, and then I start thinking about buying lottery tickets again, and then I start fantasising about what I would do if I won millions of dollars (always a fun fantasy)...

I manage to drag my thoughts away from new carpet to catch Andy telling me to listen to the sounds in the room. I hear the drier going in the laundry, and I don't even know what he says after that because I go off on a huge mental tangent about all the housework I need to do (the toilet is disgusting—my boys keep peeing all over the seat and the floor—what if someone popped in unannounced right now and needed to use the loo?), then I segue into thinking about the door-knockers who come by to try to get me to sign up to their power company or whatever, and what a terrible job that must be, and how I ducked into the pantry one time to avoid being spotted by one of them and stayed there for ages worried that they hadn't left so I ate some chippies while I was in there, and then I wonder why I keep buying mini bags of chippies when I can't resist eating them and I should buy kale chips instead but there's no way my kids are going to eat kale chips in their school lunchboxes, and suddenly I realise the audio is nearly over and Mr Ex-Circus Performer is telling me he looks forward to me coming back tomorrow for the Day Two audio.

I never do.

I don't know why. It is just a bit ... cutesy or boring or something. Just not for me. I don't feel drawn back to it. I get into the flow of life once more, super busy with all my usual jobs in the real world and online. A couple of times, I contemplate sitting back down on the sofa in the study to listen to Andy's free Day Two audio ... but I never do.

MY TOOLBOX

Recovery community

Sober treats

~~Mindfulness (Headspace)~~

'If you queef, we quit!'

I'm not sure yoga will ever make it into my toolbox, either. There's a good reason I'm anti-yoga right now. I had a bad experience with it. Like, super bad.

Back when we were living in Auckland, my sister and I attended some yoga classes together for quite a few weeks. It was her suggestion, and I thought it sounded like a good healthy, sisterly and potentially enjoyable thing to do. Boy, was I wrong! It was lovely to be attending evening classes with my sister, that much is true, but everything else about the experience was sheer hell.

I hated it. The instructor was a heavy-accented, humourless woman who ran her classes like a military operation. She had a fancy studio built in the garden at the front of her suburban home. We had very strict instructions about where we could park outside her house, very strict instructions about how to store our belongings, and very strict instructions about how to use her gear. She disliked noise of any kind and would silence us with a sharp 'Shhhh!' She was really into upside-down poses (not just downward dogs, but handstands and stuff) and balancing poses and tricky poses that were just bloody hard work, and she was militant about how perfectly we had to achieve each pose. Of course, I was far from perfect, so in order to get me perfectly positioned she used to approach me constantly, touching me to shift me around. Maybe she was approaching others as well; I can't remember. I just felt excessively manhandled. I felt like I could never get it right, because she'd forever be moving my hands a little to the left, my feet a little to the right, my shoulders around or my hips up. I felt singled-out, unfit, inflexible, out of place and usually annoyed that, at seven in the evening, I was there feeling uncomfortable in a silent and sterile garden studio instead of sitting on my sofa guzzling wine.

That was the other *major* problem with attending evening classes of any sort back then—a problem I can't blame on a perfectionist yoga instructor. At that time, I was deep in my alcohol addiction and not inclined to work any part of my body other than my arm as it lifted a wine glass to my mouth. Evenings were for enthusiastic wine consumption, not leaving my house to suffer physical discomfort and humiliation.

Actually, to be honest, I've never really been inclined to work my body much. I've got short legs, flat feet, big boobs and no natural inclination towards exercise at all. My mum still tells stories about how she used to wait at the finish line of my primary-school running races to cheer me on as I crossed last and usually in tears. I've never experienced an intoxicating endorphin rush from working out. There have been phases in my life when I've managed to go to the gym regularly and get a little bit fit, but it's always felt like a chore. It's just never been something I'm that into. Some people get sober and transfer their addiction to marathon running—how great would that be for the thighs? That has not been the case for me, though.

So yeah, downward dogs aren't my thing, and although I'm far more inclined to go out in the evenings now that I'm sober (night-time driving is one of the many joys of sobriety!), an absence of wine does not automatically lead to a sportier mindset or more flexible limbs. Despite what the Twitterati say, I'm not feeling inclined to sun salute. Not, that is, until a real-life person starts bugging me to do it as well.

I'm visiting a neighbourhood friend for lunch one weekday and as we're scoffing bacon-and-egg pies from the local bakery we watch her six-month-old baby, who is lying on the rug playing with her toes. Trying to eat her toes, to be precise.

'I love this age,' my friend says. 'She's sleeping through the night finally, but not running around creating havoc yet.'

'And so flexible!' I say. 'Imagine being able to lick your own toes like that. Actually, don't. Gross.'

'Oh, I couldn't even if I wanted to,' my friend says. 'All the sitting and breastfeeding I do has made me so stiff and inflexible. I'm feeling awful. Oh, that reminds me! I keep meaning to ask, do you want to try a yoga class at the Rec Centre with me?'

'No.' I shudder. 'I *hate* yoga. It's too scary and uptight for me.'

'It is not!' My friend laughs. She has finished her pie and is now down on the floor changing her baby's nappy. 'It's all local mums there so it can't be that fancy. Why don't we just try it once and see if we like it?' she says. 'We can stop if we don't.'

'I *hate* yoga!' I repeat firmly, still eating my pie. 'I did it in Auckland and the teacher was so strict, it was awful. And I could never do a downward dog without fanny-farting,' I admit.

She laughs. 'You mean queefing?'

'Queefing?' I splutter so hard pastry flies out of my mouth. 'What the hell is that?'

'That's the proper name for fanny-farting.'

We both crack up. The baby thinks we're hilarious and starts giggling along with us. Little does she know what joys await her…

'Seriously, though,' I say, trying to get my composure back, 'I'm not a major queefer.' I snort. 'I just did it once or twice *and* had recently had babies. I just hated every minute of the whole yoga thing.'

'Try it with me. It might be totally different and really good.'

'Or it might be hell.' I'm all set to keep resisting her suggestion but suddenly remember my new project and my promise to myself to work on changing things for the better. 'Well, I suppose a lot of people in addiction and recovery rave about yoga,' I admit. 'They're always tweeting about it and sharing photos of ridiculous poses under waterfalls.'

'There you go!' My friend is making for the rubbish bin with the dirty nappy.

'OK.' I cave. 'I'll try it. Once. But if it's awful and I fanny-fart my way through it I'm not going back.'

'Deal. If you queef, we quit!'

I can't believe I'm actually going back. But yay, me, for adding yoga to my toolbox. The Twitterati would be proud.

MY TOOLBOX

Recovery community

Sober treats

Yoga

Chapter 4

Minecraft and mindfulness
do not mix well

Heading home from my friend's I decide I'm not going to give up on my quest to try mindfulness. Just because McMindfulness from bald Andy the ex-monk didn't work for me doesn't mean there aren't other programmes around that will. I've got an hour or so before school pick-up, so I jump on Facebook and, in among the usual cat videos and recipes for jelly swirls, I see someone recommending a meditation programme run by Oprah and Deepak Chopra. Maybe this is for me? I read a book of Deepak Chopra's once (I think it was on weight-loss), and of course Oprah is the guru of all things. Maybe together these guys can sort my head out? I find their website and register via email for something-I'm-not-quite-sure-what. Nothing is free, but then sometimes they offer stuff for free... It's all rather confusing. Maybe I'll get another email when whatever-it-is is ready?

I see on the website that there's a free app, so I download it to my iPad. It's not as slick, modern and cartoony as Headspace—Oprah and Deepak favour a more mellow approach. (Their logo is a lotus flower. Enough said.) The app tells me I have access to a free audio as a welcome gift. (After that do I have to pay? Still not entirely sure how this all works.) Three o'clock is fast approaching, so I plan to listen to it later.

I race down to school to get the boys, then the next hour or so is taken up with attempting to stop them bickering, listening to their stories, feeding them snacks, doing spelling practice and getting their dinner underway. At four-thirty they're allowed some screen time, and I fight them for the iPad so I can listen to Oprah. Here's me being mindful again!

MY TOOLBOX

Recovery community

Sober treats

Yoga

Mindfulness (Oprah and Deepak)

I take the iPad into the sunroom and sit myself down on an old cane chair to listen. Turns out the free audio doesn't feature Oprah, but rather a man with an Indian accent who must be Deepak. He is saying 'I will embrace all the beauty around' over and over and over, and in the background there is some music playing.

I sit on the too-low cane chair, worrying once again that this seat is not giving me the right posture—the floral cushion sinks awfully low on the old springs so that, once again, my knees are higher than my butt. I decide to ignore this and instead shut my eyes and try to relax and focus on the audio.

The music on Deepak's app reminds me of the sort of under-water music you'd hear at the beauty therapist—all whales and chimes and floaty sounds. Talk about clichéd! But that's not the biggest problem I have. The biggest problem is the sound of a gamer playing Minecraft on YouTube that is coming from the computer in the next room, where my ten-year-old is sitting. Minecraft and mindfulness do not mix well, and despite Deepak's best efforts I am finding it hard to embrace anything other than my annoyance. Deepak's calm voice and whale music are constantly interrupted by the excited gamer next door.

'I will embrace all the beauty around...'

What I need is a crap-ton of wood...

'I will embrace all the beauty around…'

Oh, yeah. This is awesome!

'I will embrace all the beauty around…'

I need to break this down into dust…

'I will embrace all the beauty around…'

Man, I need to get some crafting tables…

'I will embrace all the beauty around…'

It's impossible to focus, and I'm frustrated as all hell. I yell at my son to turn his computer down (not a very Zen yell). He does, but I can still hear it. The beauty-therapist music grates, the gamer grates, and I decide I'm hungry, so I give up on listening to Deepak telling me to embrace the beauty all around and instead go butter some crackers.

That was over almost as soon as it began.

MY TOOLBOX

Recovery community

Sober treats

Yoga

~~Mindfulness (Oprah and Deepak)~~

I spend the rest of the evening feeling dissatisfied and pissed off. I do battle with the kids. I do battle inside my own head, telling myself to get over myself, that my problems are very First World and that I should just cheer the hell up. But I can't. Two things I've tried now haven't helped—Headspace nor Deepak and the whales. These failed attempts at something-I'm-not-sure-what are only serving to exacerbate my feelings of dissatisfaction and put me in an even grumpier mood. Why can't these things work, goddammit? I want a quick fix!

I don't get a quick fix.

I get my period instead.

It arrives right before bedtime, along with a nice crampy tummy. *Blah.* I eat some biscuits, pop some painkillers and get into bed with my iPad to spend a mindless hour or so surfing the internet, in the same Facebook–Instagram–Twitter–blog–website loop as always. Eventually, I fall asleep, but when I wake in the night to use the loo I pull a muscle in my hip, making my entire right lower back sore. It keeps me awake—as does my crampy tummy—and I lie there worrying about getting old and worrying that I'm tense and wound up and just worrying, worrying, worrying. I'm so sick of all this worrying.

I get up to fetch some more painkillers, which help with my cramps and muscle pain, and I fall back to sleep for a couple of hours.

When I wake again, I'm super grumpy, still wound up and

hassled about the world and my life. Before I even get out of bed, I reach for the iPad to check all my online spaces. I've received an email overnight from a friend who lives out of town asking me how I am, so from my prone position I reply to her, moaning about how much parenting I do and how intense it is and how I'm still sad about my step-dad being gone and life is just a bit hard and gritty right now. Woe is me.

Eventually I drag myself out of bed. While I'm grunting my way through making the school lunches, Corin employs his psychic abilities and senses that I'm not in tip-top shape. He offers to take the boys to school on his way to work. Yes! I get them packed up and out of the door while I'm still in my PJs, and once they've gone and the house is quiet I stand in the kitchen for a while before deciding to get back into bed. I *never* do this. I feel like a total slacker, but to hell with it.

As I lie there with the electric blanket on, thinking about my failed plan to learn mindfulness (or something), I suddenly remember someone on my blog mentioning Tara Brach's guided meditation podcasts, and I think *Of course!* because I love Tara Brach.

She is a psychologist and author who posts loads of free hour-long talks online that I have listened to and find really good—talks about forgiveness and kindness and so on. Some of her talks have been hugely helpful to me in times of extreme angst, but I've never listened to her twenty-minute guided meditations before because, well, meditation isn't something I do (the talks are active listening and that's why I like them). But maybe now is a good time to start. So, still lying in bed (and trying not to feel guilty because it's nine-thirty on a Friday morning and I really should be at the gym or fermenting veggies or something), I pull a Tara guided meditation up on my iPad and start listening.

Must achieve an intense, vibrating, awed silence! Must!

Tara starts talking and I think about how I love her voice and what a lovely person she would be to have over for dinner, then I wonder what sort of food she eats, then I think about how good it is that I'm lying down and not sitting on a too-low chair, but then I worry that lying down isn't the right thing to do either. So much bloody worrying all the bloody time!

I catch Tara telling me how to breathe, so I follow her instructions. I don't chant 'Ommm' like she tells me to, but I hear all the people in the room with her on the recording chanting and that is lovely, but then I start wondering about all those people and what their lives are like over in the United States, and then I hear the rubbish truck down the road tipping bottles out of neighbours' bins and I realise we forgot to put our recycling out last night—dammit, I hate it when that happens! Then I start mentally planning a trip to the dump this weekend—there's a huge pile of crap in the garage that needs to go out. Then I remember I should be listening Tara, and I try to quiet my mind, but soon I start planning some work stuff and it goes like this until I say out loud 'Sorry, Tara' and turn the meditation off with four minutes and fifty-eight seconds still to go. Fail.

I'm still feeling like being in bed is a good thing, though, and the electric blanket is incredibly toasty and warm, so rather than get up I look over to the pile of books sitting beside my bed. Right at the bottom of the pile, underneath a Chelsea Winter cookbook and some random parenting book my sister lent me, is a dusty copy of *Eat, Pray, Love* by Elizabeth Gilbert. I bought it at a school gala and started reading it ages ago, but for some reason never finished it. I grab it and resume reading where I left off. Oh, look at that! She is writing about trying to learn how to meditate while at an ashram in India, and about her monkey brain and how she has to fight against her thoughts and ego, and her busy, busy mind and the battles that go on in her head. (Hello?! Yes, Liz, that's me too! Maybe we could be besties!) And then suddenly she writes about an intense moment that occurs for her while she is trying to meditate when all the chattering, negative thoughts in her mind scatter and a regal silence follows. She calls it an 'intense, vibrating, awed silence'. I put the book down and stare at the ceiling.

Oh. My. God. I want this so bad. I want an intense, vibrating, awed silence. I want it desperately!

Liz's vivid description combined with my desperation give me a little surge of energy and renewed determination—enough to get me out of bed, into the shower and dressed. I must keep going with my plan. Must achieve an intense, vibrating, awed silence! Must!

I go down to the study, sit at the computer, open up Google and type 'learn mindfulness' in the search bar. I land upon a site called Mindful (mindful.org). They have a free regular newsletter, so I fill in the required fields to register for it. I know this sounds like nothing much, but it actually does feel quite significant—like I'm doing something positive to alter my state of mind. Even just this teeny-tiny step has me feeling encouraged.

Instantly I receive an email confirmation with a friendly 'Welcome!', and attached to it is a document called '5 Techniques for a Mindful Day'. At the top it says: 'Mindfulness is a natural human ability. It's also something you can improve with practice. When you create ways in your day to slow down and be fully present, you can reconnect with this basic but transformative quality.'

OK, bring it on! I want to create ways in my day to slow down and be present. I do! The techniques read as pretty uncomplicated.

Technique One is about sitting and getting your posture right and relaxing.

Technique Two is about settling into a comfortable position and scanning your entire body, slowly lingering on the different sensations in each area as you go.

Technique Three is a ten-minute tea-making ritual—slowly making a good cup of tea and being aware of every step, being a part of it all, even when the water is boiling. Just 'be with the water boiling', and then sip and really notice the taste and sensation of the tea. (Not sure how to 'be with the water boiling' but anyway…)

Technique Four is a stress-busting technique that has you stopping, breathing, observing your thoughts and emotions. Stop, breathe, observe, proceed.

Technique Five is about mindfully listening, about being fully present with another person.

I read through this list, then before leaving the computer I navigate to the public library website and its online catalogue to search for some books. First I go for three on mindfulness that have been recommended to me by blog readers (they know all my woes). The first is an anthology of essays on mindfulness, the second a sort of memoir–journalism crossover by an American TV reporter (apparently he had a panic attack live on air before he discovered the joys of meditation—sounds juicy) and the third is some sort of eight-week plan to turn me into a chilled-out, happy camper. I find them all, place reserves and organise for them to be sent to my local library branch (the eight-week guide is popular—I'll have to wait a while for that one). Then, on a whim, I reserve some books on sugar because I know that's a big area of concern for me as well.

Next, I go to YouTube and find a clip of Dan Harris's live-on-air panic attack. It is pretty uncomfortable to watch. Poor dude! No wonder he turned to meditation after that embarrassment.

After all this effort—well, OK, not *that* much effort, but some—I decide to go and lie on the sofa and start watching the Real Housewives of Somewhere fight about who-said-what-to-whom. At 3 pm I get the kids from school, then work like a demon until 8 pm when, lo and behold, I'm back on the sofa binging on chocolate.

Is this a happy sober life?

I do manage some nice thinking-about-nothing-but-my-belly-button moments

I wake at six-thirty the next morning feeling sick and guilty about all the chocolate I ate the night before. The idea pops into my head that I could try the 'body-scan' technique from the mindfulness newsletter I got yesterday. I could lie still on my back and go around my body thinking about all the different areas, bringing awareness to each. (Is that what you do?) That would be something proactive, wouldn't it? But then Corin rolls over and flicks on the radio, and our youngest son arrives to snuggle in with us, all full of chatter about his dreams, then our middle son arrives, and he gets into bed as well even though he's quite big now, and suddenly we're all squirming bodies and noise and my mindful moment is lost.

But after getting everyone off to school and work and doing some jobs around the house I realise I'm at a point in my day where I could choose to sit at the computer and do some work… or I could (*gulp*) actually sit down and do a body-scan. Holy shit. This is it. I'm actually going to do it!

First, I print off the mindfulness newsletter from yesterday and head into the TV room to sit on the edge of the sofa. Is this a good spot to sit in? No, I don't think so—too squishy. Maybe cross-legged on the floor would be better? I grab one cushion to plonk my bum on, and two more to put under each knee, then hold my newsletter up and read about what to do.

I'll start with Technique One, I tell myself, *because it's only three minutes long and if I can't sit for three minutes then I have a serious problem.* The newsletter tells me that meditation begins and ends in the body, and that I need to take the time to pay attention to where I am and what's going on, and that starts with being aware of my body. 'That very act can be calming, since our body has internal rhythms that help it relax if we give it a chance.' Oooh, internal rhythms. That sounds groovy.

I read on. They tell me to take a seat (have done that already and the cushions are nice and soft, although maybe I should have bigger ones under each knee?), straighten my upper body—not stiff, just straight—(I straighten but try not to stiffen, flexing my back up and down, and wonder, *Is this straight or stiff?*), position my hands and arms comfortably, then drop my gaze, close my eyelids and relax. I drop the newsletter and let my hands rest on my knees, then I lower my eyelids and relax.

For about a nanosecond. Or maybe a bit longer. Five nanoseconds.

After my five nanoseconds, I grab the newsletter again to read what it says to do next. Nothing! That was it! Just take time to settle myself into a comfortable seated position and relax—that was Technique One. It definitely didn't take me three minutes, but what the hell. The newsletter says I could stop now or move into some mindfulness practice. Well, hell, let's go for broke, eh!

Technique Two is the body-scan one. This is just an extension of what I'm already doing: sitting comfortably, so I feel supported and relaxed, then bringing awareness to my whole body, piece by piece. They give me a helpful order to do this in: toes, feet, legs, pelvis, abdomen, lower back, upper back, et cetera, et cetera, right through my whole body. They tell me to linger on each body part and notice the different sensations.

If I find my mind has wandered, I have to bring it back to the last body part I was on.

So I launch into it and I try really hard to focus on each body part. Really, I do. But my mind is wandering like buggery. I try to pull it back each time, and I do manage some nice thinking-about-nothing-but-my-belly-button moments, but by the time I arrive at my back the only sensation I am aware of is a dull ache, so I call it quits.

I'm a little bit proud of myself for actually doing something concrete, but overall my main feeling is that I was doing it all wrong and it was a big failed attempt. It just didn't really feel like anything much—I certainly didn't achieve an intense, vibrating, awed silence à la Liz Gilbert. *I must be doing it all wrong*, I decide as I get up off the floor and get on with some jobs around the house.

But something interesting happens a short while later...

Chapter 5

It's a tiny little moment, but it feels rather significant

It's just a small thing, but it's interesting nonetheless. I'm outside later in the day, hanging out the washing and thinking about an email I just received from a writer in the UK. She's setting up an alcohol-free reviewer group to help authors get feedback on their manuscripts, and wants me to join it. Should I? The sun is shining and I'm distracted by the annoying hot stones under my feet. They're hot—like, super hot. Too-hot-to-stand-on-in-bare-feet hot. But I've got bare feet, so I'm jiggling around, trying to keep my feet moving so they don't get too sore while also thinking about my emails.

Suddenly I remember the body-awareness thing from my time on the cushion earlier, so I stop thinking about the UK author's request and think about my feet instead. I let myself become super aware of my hot feet, and my mind kind of goes quiet. I focus on my hot feet—like, really focus. I think about my hot feet and concentrate on feeling the heat, and my mind is quiet.

It's a tiny little moment, but it feels rather significant and, to be honest, nice. It's nice to not be thinking about work stuff and just feeling my feet.

I decide the hot stones aren't that bad and play a little game to see how long I can stand still without needing to move. I discover I can bear the heat for longer than I thought, and the hot stones are actually rather lovely.

I finish hanging out the washing and head inside, aware of the fact I did something a little different and it feels kinda nice. Subtle but freeing somehow to not just be thinking about work stuff.

A little later, I'm standing at the kitchen sink washing some dishes and I'm worrying about a friend's relationship with her husband, which seems a little strained. Suddenly I catch myself worrying and again remember about the body-awareness thing. I look down and, instead of continuing to worry about the state of my friend's marriage, I look hard at what my hands are doing. They're busy with the pots and pans in the full, soapy sink. Look at my busy hands efficiently washing pots! I probably wash dishes with my bright-green rubber gloves three or four times a day, yet I've never really noticed how they look moving away in the suds.

I slow my hands down and notice the fingers covered in green rubber moving in and out of the water, holding a red dish brush. They look rather nice! Add the yellow dish-cloth into the mix and I've got a wonderland of colour. Sounds weird, but it's quite cool and also satisfying. I slow down and observe my hands closely. I start to kind of enjoy washing the dishes. It's far more enjoyable than worrying about the state of someone else's marriage.

Is this mindfulness? I think it might be.

It feels nice. These are only small steps that I'm taking, but there's definitely something there. Certainly enough that I feel confident to mentally put mindfulness back in my toolbox. I might only be scratching the surface, but it's happening. It is.

MY TOOLBOX

Recovery community
Sober treats
Mindfulness
Yoga

Nobody wants to see a lumpy, knicker-wearing housewife trying to go all Zen in her living room

The next day I do nothing. Well, nothing mindful anyway. Nothing towards my goal of pure, blissful nirvana. I run around like a blue-arsed fly, busy with the kids, busy with the house, busy online, busy thinking, busy snacking, busy, busy, busy. Who knows where my mind is at, but it's not focusing on hot stones or rubber gloves, that's for sure.

I have an empty 40-minute window in the middle of the day when I could choose to do something mindful, meditation-y, whatever-it-is-I'm-trying-to-do-y, but I don't. I fill those 40 minutes with some fiddling around trying to resize a photo for my blog, replying to a couple of emails (there's one from the colleague who I am finding it tricky to work with, which activates my stress a bit), and interacting with members on Living Sober.

Then Friday rolls around. It's yet another busy day, as per usual, but after I post a mocktail recipe on my Facebook page I again find myself with a 45-minute window of free time before school pick-up. This time I resist getting sucked into an online vortex of celebrity gossip and local news. Instead, I grab my printed mindfulness newsletter and put my cushions back down on the floor and try to sit on them with my legs crossed.

It's hard, because my jeans are tight—like, *super* tight! So I get up and wrestle them off before sitting back down with just my knickers on. Then I realise I need to wee so I pop to the loo quickly, then return and sit back down cross-legged again. I start by repeating the three-minute posture practice from a couple of days ago, which just involves taking the time to sit properly, back straight but not stiff, arms by my sides and hands resting where they fall on my legs, gaze lowered, relaxing...

It's sort of nice being back in that position. Actually, that's a lie. It's not really. Cross-legged sitting is hell, and it's quite hard to focus on my posture because I'm hyper-aware that if anyone came to the window right now they'd get a full view of me in my smalls. And nobody wants to see a lumpy, knicker-wearing housewife trying to go all Zen in her living room. Although, on second thought, maybe that'd get rid of the door-knockers once and for all!

I try hard to push self-conscious thoughts out of my mind and instead get my posture sorted, then start to do the body-scan, going around each area of my body, bringing consciousness to each body part. I do OK going around each part (still a bit of an ache in my back when I get there, so I straighten myself a little and it feels better). By the time I've made my way around my entire body (with a lot of mind wandering in between), I've forgotten the possibility of being caught out in my knickers, am warm from the sun coming through the windows, and feel rather relaxed. I decide to give my stiff knees a break by stretching my legs out in front of me and lying back on the rug. One of my library books has arrived and I have it next to me, so pick it up to read a bit. It's an anthology of essays called *The Mindfulness Revolution*, edited by Barry Boyce. (I later find out he is also editor-in-chief of the mindful.org site whose newsletter I subscribed to.)

In the introduction Barry says, 'By taking time away from the pressures and needs of daily life to work only on mindfulness, with no other project at hand, we refresh our ability to be mindful when we return to our everyday activities.'

Ah, OK . . . So this is like the other day when I sat to do a formal meditation-type thing for a bit, then later found myself really noticing the hot stones under my feet and the look of my hands in the soapy sink. It's good that Barry is reassuring me that my goal doesn't necessarily have to be an intense, vibrating, awed silence or some other kind of far-fetched meditation achievement. My goal can just be bringing attention to my body when I'm taking time to sit and breathe, then remembering to do it later when I'm feeling busy. But is he telling me that I have to do the formal sit-down every day in order to remember to notice the little things when I'm back at work?

I feel stressed about this, which kind of defeats the purpose of it all. I don't want to feel pressured to have to find time every day to sit and focus on my breath or body (or whatever).

Honestly, I don't really want to do this. It's boring! It feels like a hassle to have to find the time to do it every day on top of all the other demands on my time. Can't I just skip the formal sit-downs and try to remember to focus on my body parts while I'm busy doing things (rather than being lost in thought)?

I'm not sure I can. I'm not sure about any of this. I've still got this notion that I need to be striving hard to do something formal every day, and it's making me feel pressured, like if I don't do it I'm failing in my mission to really nail this mindfulness stuff.

There's no way I'm going to sit on the floor cross-legged when I could be judging movie stars' outfits

Whatever is required, I do nothing much of it at all over the weekend. Saturday, I do zero of a sit-down-and-be-quiet-and-mindful nature. There's a moment in the afternoon when everyone else in the family is watching TV and it occurs to me that I *could* take myself into the study, shut the door, sit cross-legged and focus on my breath and do a body-scan...but I dismiss that thought and instead find myself at the laundry sink scrubbing stains out of white rugby shorts.

Sunday, I manage to sit myself down cross-legged on the bedroom rug and listen to my breath and start with a bit of a body-scan, but I only last for about 90 seconds because it just feels dumb. But I've committed myself, and the stubborn part of me is telling me to keep going until something happens. I know other people can get something out of this and I'm determined to see what it is they're on about.

Monday rolls around and it's Oscars day. I love the Academy Awards! There's no way I'm going to sit on the floor cross-legged when I could be judging movie stars' outfits.

I watch E! channel's red-carpet coverage while dipping in and out of my library book, and a passage grabs my attention for long enough that I stop wondering why Gwyneth Paltrow has planted a giant pink flower on her shoulder. This passage is from a chapter written by a Joseph Goldstein, co-founder of the Insight Meditation Society in Massachusetts, and he's saying, 'Have you ever stopped to consider what a thought is—not the content but the very nature of thought itself?'

No, Joseph. Now that you ask, I haven't.

'Few people really explore the question, "What is a thought?" What is this phenomenon that occurs so many times a day and to which we pay so little attention?'

Right now, on glancing up at the TV, I'm thinking, *Why has J-Lo dressed herself up like a Disney princess?* But her ginormous, poofy dress doesn't hold my attention for long... This talk of the nature of thought has piqued my interest. I tear my eyes from the screen to read on.

> Not being aware of the thoughts that arise in our minds or of the very nature of thought itself allows thoughts to dominate our lives. Telling us to do this, say that, go here, go there— thoughts often drive us like we're their servants. Unnoticed, they have great power. But when we pay attention, when we observe thoughts as they arise and pass away, we begin to see their essentially empty nature. They arise as little energy bubbles in the mind rather than reified expressions of a self.

How utterly fascinating. He's right. I have never explored the nature of thought itself. I have had people say to me 'thoughts aren't facts' but I've never really known what they meant. I once asked a very wise woman with over twenty years of sobriety under her belt what her best tool was for dealing with life in the raw and she replied, 'Not believing everything I think.' I remember nodding sagely at her as though I knew exactly what she meant, but in truth she might as well have been speaking Chinese for all I understood. Maybe she was already attuned to this concept that thoughts are nothing more than empty little energy bubbles? Well, this is all new to me! I feel like I'm just scratching the surface of some sort of radical concept here, but in no way have I got my head around it yet.

Are thoughts truly empty? I feel like my thoughts are rich and full and interesting. They're *me*. I *am* my thoughts. My thoughts lead me and guide me and make sense of the world for me. My thoughts help me to process stuff, to explain things to my kids, to communicate with people and to write. It's my thinking that helped me realise I had a problem with alcohol and got me sober, for goodness' sake! And I wouldn't be exploring all this mindfulness stuff if I hadn't thought to do it.

What else am I if I'm not my thoughts?

Chapter 6

It's amazing how boring my thoughts are a lot of the time

I'm intrigued enough by this talk of energy puffs in the mind that I do actually manage to sit quietly for a few minutes after *Birdman* has won Best Picture, the family is fed, the house is tidied, the washing is folded, clean sheets have been put on our youngest son's bed (he's started wetting again—*gah!*), I've gone online to interact with the community at Living Sober, helped a few members with their forgotten passwords, sent a group email organising my sister's birthday present, emailed the Scout leaders to confirm a camp for our eldest, liked a few posts on Instagram, accepted a few friend requests on Facebook, paid a bill and visited the *Daily Mail* website to see how the world is judging Gwyneth and J-Lo's dresses.

Once I've torn my eyes from the screen I sit down cross-legged on the bedroom rug and shut my eyes and try to ignore the chattering coming from Corin and the boys outside on the trampoline. Unlike the other times I've done this sitting-down thing (is it meditation? I feel embarrassed to say it is! And it doesn't feel like it), this time I'm not desperately trying to achieve a quiet mind or do the perfect body-scan or anything. I just try to observe these little energy puffs of mine to see what it is I'm thinking about.

It's interesting. The process that is, not my thoughts. My thoughts are not interesting in the slightest.

At first there is nothing there—or at least there's too much there. Inside my head it's murky and noisy and a big blur. I can't tell what is going on; it's just very noisy and messy. I sit and wait to see what it is I'm thinking about but there's nothing discernible, just a big noisy jumble. I try to focus on my breath and I do that for a brief instant, then without even noticing it I'm off mentally planning school lunches for tomorrow ... and suddenly I realise what I'm doing, and it's clear what I'm thinking about. *I'm thinking about taking bread rolls out of the freezer!* I think and then it all goes quiet. Weird. Noticing what I was thinking about made it stop. That's interesting.

I wait again, eyes still shut. It's all blurry and noisy and indiscernible once more . . . then things start to calm a little and I forget what I'm doing, then I realise that I am wondering whether I should put night nappies back on our youngest. I notice the thought about nappies that my brain has formed and I think, *I'm thinking about nappies!* It feels like a little triumph that I noticed the thought so clearly . . . but again, once I have that noticing-the-thought thought, it goes quiet for me internally.

So then I think, *Oh, time to focus on my breath!* and I do that for probably three seconds before I go off on another mental tangent, and this time I get completely hooked by the thoughts and forget to notice them; I just merrily think away. I stay completely caught up and lost in my thoughts for a while (no idea how long because I'm so caught up by the energy bubbles in my mind) until my attention turns to the sound of our eldest boy calling out to me as he heads down the hallway towards the bedroom. I quickly jump up so he doesn't catch me sitting on the rug and ask what the hell I am doing. Quiet time is over.

But I have to admit that, even though I got hooked and taken away by my thoughts, I'm a little psyched about this new concept of my thoughts being energy puffs. Sounds kind of kooky, but it feels quite revolutionary for me. I've never really paused to notice what I am thinking. I mean, I'm aware what I'm thinking all the time, but I'm usually just going with the thoughts rather than pausing and really noticing them as 'things'. What sort of 'things' they are and where this newfound awareness is going to take me, I have no idea.

I've since read a lot about the nature of thoughts and am much more attuned to the truth that they are nothing but hollow little energy puffs in the mind—sometimes useful and called for, other times useless and unwanted. The author and meditation teacher Sharon Salzberg (who looks super friendly and cuddly and I'd love to have a cup of tea with her one day) describes them like this:

> Thoughts moving through your mind are like clouds moving across the sky. They are not the sky, and the sky remains unchanged by them. The way to be with them is just to watch them go by. Thoughts and feelings move through our minds and constantly change; they're not who we are. They're just what we're thinking and feeling in the moment.

And Dr Dan Siegel, co-director of UCLA's Mindful Awareness Research Center, says in his book *Mindsight*:

> The mind is like the ocean ... no matter what the surface conditions are like, whether it's smooth or choppy ... deep in the ocean it's tranquil and serene. From the depths of the ocean, you can look towards the surface and simply notice the activities there, just as from the depths of the mind you can

look upward towards all that activity of the mind—thoughts, feelings, sensations, and memories.

Right now, following my eldest back towards the kitchen, for the first time since embarking on this new project, I feel quite jazzed and certainly curious to explore more. I'm so jazzed I get out of bed early the next morning to do a mindful sit-down. Jeepers, who am I?!

It's 6.50 am and the house is still quiet, which is rare (the kids are usually up by now), so still in my jazzed and curious state I get out of bed, put a sweatshirt on and go down to the living room to sit cross-legged on a cushion with my hands resting on my knees and my eyes shut.

I don't really know what happens while I'm sitting there. I think about lots of inane things and sometimes remember to notice what I am thinking about and maybe I remember to bring my attention back to my breath once or twice, but mostly I just merrily think about stuff, including the fact that I'm not that comfortable sitting cross-legged and I've got a bursting bladder ... so after about three minutes (at the most) I get up to go relieve myself and a child arrives upstairs and we're into the day.

OK, it's not much ... but good on me for getting out of bed with the best of intentions.

After a full morning (during which, despite being busy with

household jobs and writing work, I still manage to waste time on Instagram and overthink a few troubling things), I decide to do another sit-down. Back on to the living-room rug I go, with my legs crossed but no tight jeans hampering my posture this time.

I'm still not entirely sure what exactly I am meant to be doing, although I've got the idea now to just observe my thoughts and try to focus my attention on my breath or body parts. I do this. It goes OK. It's pretty peaceful, actually. I am aware, though, that my mind is pretty busy. *I should open the windows before I leave to let the flies out* and *Must remember to take the mince out of the freezer* are the types of illuminating thoughts I'm having. Boooooring. Honestly, it's amazing how boring my thoughts are a lot of the time. I've never noticed before! I'm aware of all the angsty, fraught thoughts, but not the ho-hum, incredibly boring thoughts I have.

But are they totally useless? I mean it *would* be a good idea to open the windows before I go out so we're not bombarded with flies while eating our dinner, and I *do* need to take the mince out so we've actually got some dinner to eat. These thoughts may be inane, but they're necessary for a busy housewife to have, otherwise how would I keep things ticking over for everyone day after day?

This second sit-down of the day probably lasts a good twelve minutes, but I have to be honest: it feels totally dumb. I don't know what the hell I'm doing, there's no great revelations coming at me or incredible sensations being felt, and I'm struggling to see the point.

If I knew then that this was going to be my last self-directed meditation for months, maybe I would have appreciated it more. But, unfortunately, life gets in the way.

I can't shake the feeling that there's some secret to be found behind my eyelids

A fellow mum sends me a snippy message about something that has gone down on a playdate. She is not happy about it. I hate this kind of shit. It stresses me out! I find it awkward and uncomfortable. I respond to her message—trying to be lighthearted and conciliatory—but I don't hear back from her. It feels unresolved.

And so I think about it. *A lot.* I ruminate about what has occurred. Thoughts are flying at me and I'm not even trying to notice them in any sort of 'mindful' way. I just let them form and take roost.

I can't believe she's reacted like this.

What was she thinking when she sent that?

I am so offended.

She mustn't like me much.

This isn't that big a deal!

Maybe no one likes me . . .
I wish this had never happened.
So RUDE not to reply to my reply.
I wish I hadn't replied.
I should have replied differently.
Maybe I should have called her instead.
This is ridiculous.

I get quite wound up about the whole incident and struggle to get it out of my mind for the next few days. I go out for coffee with a couple of long-time friends and chew it over with them. We analyse what happened on the playdate. We analyse the other mother's reaction and her message to me. We analyse my response to her message. We analyse her lack of response.

'I'm so offended by this and I don't know why! I wish I just didn't care. Why am I taking it so personally?' I wail, slurping my decaf flat white.

'Some people are just blunt like that,' one friend says supportively. 'Do you know her very well?'

'Not really,' I admit. 'We've only met a couple of times.'

'Well, there you go!'

'But isn't that all the more reason to make things super friendly?' I moan, with a mouthful of almond croissant. 'Like, wouldn't you reply to make sure things were cool? I would always reply!'

'Me too,' says my other friend. 'I'd be desperately trying to make it amicable.'

'Oh, same here,' I mumble, shovelling the final piece of pastry into my mouth, before changing the subject to talk about their new puppies. They are happy to oblige as they are both obsessed with the new furry additions to their families.

My friends are lovely, but all this additional analysis of the incident isn't helping me get over it. In my wound-up state I decide to reignite the internal argument with my colleague. Nothing new has happened in real life, but in my head we are still locked in a bitter and tense discussion. Round and round the same old arguments I go. I forget everything mindful I'm supposed to be learning. I forget about thoughts being empty energy puffs. I forget to notice what my hands or feet are doing. I go back into autopilot mode, being led around by my busy, floating head.

Any free brain time I have (in the shower in the morning, doing the dishes, driving the car), I spend thinking about fraught things that are occurring in my life. The rest of the time I am working (and wasting time) online, and doing all my other housewife-y jobs.

On top of all this, I'm about to head down country to deliver two talks about my drinking and recovery story. I've done a little bit of public speaking and don't usually get too nervous about it, but these groups want me to talk for an hour with no PowerPoint presentation, which means I won't have any slides to prompt me along with my story. I need to do lots of extra practice to memorise the flow. Any spare alone time I have, I'm standing up in the study, performing my talk to an invisible audience.

Of course, all this extra stress and busyness and brain noise just further cement my disinclination to spend any time on my new mindfulness research project—I'm far too busy for any of that. I don't want to sit on the bloody floor, focusing on my breath and trying to ignore the buzzing flies when I've got so much going on.

If nothing else, at least the tiny amount of mindfulness work I've already done is making me more aware of what I'm thinking most of the time. But being hyper-aware that I am worrying about my talks and ruminating over tricky interpersonal scenarios doesn't help to progress or solve any of it.

I do at least manage to find a little free time to start reading the second of my library books, which has just come in. It's called *10% Happier* and is by the North American TV reporter and panic-attack guy, Dan Harris. It's really interesting—part journalism, part memoir—but reading him report on feeling an 'amazing', 'thrilling' and 'exhilarating' mental breakthrough when meditating one day only serves to make me even more despondent, like there's some incredible experience only I'm missing out on. (Admittedly, this breakthrough came to him after he'd spent hours meditating while on a retreat, but still.)

Maybe sitting down on the floor to focus on my breath or watch my thoughts or whatever would help in this time of stress? But, every time I consider doing it, I decide I can't be bothered. It seems pointless taking time out of my busy day to sit and do something that, while vaguely interesting, is not really giving me any immediate rewards. I also have a deep-down feeling that I was kind of failing at it anyway. My mind always wanders like buggery, and I don't feel that happy or comfortable in that cross-legged, eyes-closed position.

I take my first library book to the hairdressers. After we've had a chat about what I want to do with my hair ('a trim and some highlights, thanks'), the hairdresser puts the cape around my shoulders and asks me what I'm reading. I feel a bit embarrassed showing her the cover of *The Mindfulness Revolution*. There's obviously still a big part of me that thinks any kind of inner work is to be scorned. She asks me about it and I don't know what to say without sounding like a dick, so I stutter, 'I'm just interested to find out what it is, because everyone is going on about it. You know, being aware of your thoughts and stuff. But I still don't really get it...'

I shouldn't have worried. As she starts putting foils in my hair, she proceeds to tell me all about her mum back in Wales, who has been meditating for years.

'For my entire childhood, every now and then out of the

blue she'd just say, "If you'll excuse me for a minute, darling, I'm going to sit for a moment." And then she'd close her eyes and meditate.'

'For real? Right in front of you?' I can't believe it! 'What does she look like when she's doing it?'

'Just all calm and serene.'

We both chuckle away merrily at the mental image of her mum meditating so boldly in front of her daughter.

'One time we went on holiday together to Spain and the flight got delayed. We had to sit for ages at the departure gate and Mum sat upright in front of all the other passengers and meditated. I was mortified!'

'You're joking!'

We both crack up at this point. The audacity of the woman!

But part of me feels desperate to know what my hairdresser's mum is experiencing. I can't shake the feeling that there's some secret to be found behind my eyelids. But so far it's totally eluding me...

What would thinking of myself as a bus do to actually change anything in real life?

A few hours later, I'm with the kids at the rugby club rooms registering them for the upcoming winter season. It's a chaotic scene. Kids are crazy excited, running around like wild things. Parents are busy trying to fill in forms, buy regulation socks and get their manic offspring on to scales to be weighed. I do all that is required for my rugby-playing sons, then bump into a friend I haven't seen for ages. We embrace and step to the side of the melee for a catch-up.

She admires my new hairdo; I admire her dress. She tells me about her promotion; I tell her about my upcoming talks. She tells me her sister's been sick; I tell her my step-father died. She moans about grumpy colleagues; I moan about snippy mothers. She tells me she's trying to avoid wheat; I tell her I'm in a constant battle with sugar. She confides she's feeling a bit stressed and tired; I do the same. Then I blurt out that I'm exploring mindfulness.

'I've just done a course on it!' she says. 'Through my work.'

'No way!' Maybe I shouldn't feel so embarrassed about this after all. 'It's quite a radical concept, isn't it?' I still don't know exactly how to identify what it is. 'You know, thinking about your thoughts and stuff.'

'For sure,' she says. 'One of the main things we were taught was that labelling your thoughts is a big step in diminishing their power.'

That's a new one. 'What, like "happy" or "sad" and stuff?' I don't quite understand what she means.

'Not that so much as identifying which parts of you they

are coming from. Like, "This is the incessant worrier in me talking." Or, "This is the insecure professional."'

'Or, "This is the uptight mother!"'

We both laugh. We can see our kids playing roughly on the equipment in the corner of the room but pretend not to notice. So much for being uptight mothers.

'They said if you can identify which part of you the thought is coming from,' my friend goes on, 'and label it as such, you can take some of its power away. You can tell that version of yourself that they have been heard, thank you very much for their input, now they can move away.'

Whooping and hollering comes from the corner.

'That's really interesting,' I say.

'I know. Cool, eh? Oh, and they said to think of yourself as a bus and realise that your different emotions take turns driving the bus. Sometimes you have to take the steering wheel off different emotions if they've been in control for too long.'

'Oh, I like that bus analogy.'

'Yeah, it's a goodie. STOP DOING THAT!'

The play-fighting has gone too far and my friend dashes away to intervene before her son breaks something—like his leg.

I stand where I am for a moment longer, letting her words sink in.

I like this concept a whole lot. Maybe I can stop some of the overthinking I do if I label my thoughts and then send them to the back of the bus. I could think, *Thank you, insecure writer inside me, you have been heard. Thank you for your input. Now let go of the wheel and go to the back seat.* Then maybe I'd chill out. That would be pretty cool!

But what would that achieve? It might stop me worrying for a while but it wouldn't actually do anything to improve the situation, would it? What would thinking of myself as a bus do to actually change anything in real life? There's more to ponder here.

No time for that now, though. My phone dings with a text message at the same time as I catch sight of my boys punching each other. I check the message and see it's from my neighbourhood friend: *Yoga next Wednesday, 7 pm!*

Oh, gawd. Do I have to go through with that?

Yes, I tell myself firmly, and quickly type *Cool* and throw in a devil-face emoji just to give her a bit of attitude. I'm still not convinced that yoga is something I'll ever get into.

I head over to round the boys up and get them home.

My friend catches me for a hug goodbye on the way out ('Great catching up!' 'Let's do coffee.' 'Yes, definitely.') and we're off.

Our conversation about buses and honestly labelling thoughts lingers with me on the way home. I start thinking again about the mum with whom I had the unsatisfying text-message exchange. (I had expected to see her at the rugby registration but didn't, thankfully.) The same well-worn thoughts come flying at me.

I can't believe she reacted like that.

What was she thinking when she sent that?

I am so offended.

Does she even like me?

She mustn't like me much.

Then I remember the conversation I just had with my friend, and a new, honest thought forms.

This is the insecure person inside of you talking.

Something shifts a little.

I start to wonder if all of my internal drama about what occurred with this mum is based on my own insecurities. Have I created all of this angst, rather than it being her fault? Being black-and-white about labelling my thoughts as coming from the insecure part of me is changing my perspective.

Then another thought pops into my head, totally unbidden.

She's not thinking about you at all.

Suddenly something quite dramatic happens inside me.

Chapter 7

'Everything is fluid.
Let it go.'

I can feel it very clearly. This is a big shift—almost like a release. I feel calmer all of a sudden. My inner dialogue shifts away from the uptight thoughts I've been repeating over and over for days about this mum, and a new dialogue takes shape.

She's probably crazy busy in her own life.

She probably didn't mean much by her words.

Who knows what's happening with her?

Whatever she's feeling, that's her business.

This isn't a big deal at all.

I don't have to care.

I'm not thinking these thoughts in an uptight way, nor am I thinking about her in a mean way, like *She's being a callous cow*; I'm thinking it all in a detached and quite calm way. Somehow I've managed to totally release all my worked-up angst simply by recognising my own part in it. I've made this a much bigger deal that I needed to. I can choose to let it go.

So I do.

With this simple labelling of my thoughts as coming from the insecure part of me, I release all of my angst regarding the incident. I could probably still take this woman's original message as having been a bit abrupt, but I let it go completely and honestly don't care at all anymore. It goes! I hardly think of it ever again.

Months later, I bump into the mum in question at a social event, and we have a nice-enough chat. I can see that she is busy and preoccupied with her own life, and she doesn't seem to harbour any ill feelings towards me or my son. I secretly feel a bit foolish knowing I created such a big drama with her in my own head, when no drama existed in reality at all!

I still remember this scenario often, as it was a classic case of me grasping on to a situation to create a drama out of an incident that really didn't warrant such a major reaction. I would like to say that this is the only time I have held on to something like this, but it's not. It is, however, the first time I am able to actively process and settle such a situation for myself in a way that is very honest, calming and freeing.

Some months later, I listen to a podcast in which mindfulness expert Joseph Goldstein talks about this notion of grasping on to things both good and bad (like this imagined drama), and I totally relate to what he says. He explains that grasping is a natural tendency of the mind: we feel things, or things happen, and it's natural for us to grab them with our minds and dwell on them or wish they'd either go away or stay there forever. But, he says, that always runs foul for us, because life is fluid: *nothing* stays the same and *everything* is in a constant state of change. He says we have the ability to work at becoming more fluid ourselves, and we are therefore able to learn to let things go—and this applies to both positive and negative things.

> It's so easy to become attached to a wonderful experience. I mean, even a genuinely transforming one, but then we become attached to it, forgetting that everything is subject to the law of change and it will inevitably change and that the fact that it changes is not incorrect practice but holding on to it is incorrect practice. And so, learning just to be with it as it unfolds, knowing that the peak experiences are not going to last in the same way but that they can still have an impact in our lives.

I love this notion of fluidity. I find it reassuring when I'm feeling sad about a good time ending, and calming when something gritty happens. If I remember to remain fluid, I'm far less likely to get stuck in my head and create a huge internal drama like I did with this mum.

Nowadays, if I ever find myself starting to get wound up, creating a huge narrative in my head about something that someone else has said or done, I remember the thought process that freed me from the over-the-top internal angst I created with this woman.

Don't grasp, Lotta! I'll tell myself. *Everything is fluid. Let it go.*

I also try to be honest about the shit I'm bringing to the table, because my own issues and emotional baggage are always playing a part. If I can be honest about that, it usually helps. I also try to remind myself that other people have their own shit going on (most of which I probably have no idea about). Most of all, I remember that I'm in control of the bus and therefore have the power to choose how much airtime I give any situation in my head.

This doesn't mean I don't ever get wound up about instances involving other people anymore—oh, gawd, if only—but nowadays I'm able to process issues more quickly than I used to be able to, hopefully without grasping on to them and unnecessarily amplifying them internally for weeks on end.

Anyway, at that moment, I feel quite lifted by this little mental turnaround I have managed to achieve with regards to this other mum, and I feel quite happy and free as I make my way home with the boys. Over the next few days, I work hard to remind myself not to get wound up in my head, and to stay focused on what is *actually* happening to me in the present moment rather than on unhelpful thoughts. As a result, I definitely feel calmer and more at peace. I do still have butterflies in my tummy, but they're easily explained: I'm about to dive back into the black abyss of hell masquerading as a yoga class.

There was no unwanted air in unwanted places for me tonight

'I don't want to go to a stupid, dumb yoga class!' I'm moaning to Corin as we stand in the bedroom. 'I don't know what to wear.'

He's just home from work and is getting out of his suit. I'm staring into my wardrobe in a state of despair. I don't own any fancy yoga duds or active wear of any description. 'Can I just not go?'

'Just wear something comfy,' he says, before abandoning me for the kitchen, in search of food.

I look at my watch. The class starts in twenty minutes. It's too late to pull out now. My friend would kill me! I pull on a baggy pair of old leggings (hand-me-downs from my mum) and a big, floppy T-shirt, then race out of the house with a quick 'See you soon' to the boys, who are all flopped in front of the television.

Tonight's yoga class is being held in the local rec centre, which is just three blocks down on the very same road as our house. Really, it couldn't be any closer unless it was in my living room. I drive 40 seconds down the road (a different human would probably have walked) quickly find a park and race to meet my friend out the front. She hands me her spare yoga mat (why does she have two yoga mats? Is she secretly a super-yogi?), and we head inside to the front counter to pay the casual rate for a one-off class before making our way to the room where it's being held. It's in the big room at the front of the centre, where they usually hold antenatal classes or karate. Tonight it's full with fifteen or so people—mostly women—sitting around on yoga mats. There's not a lot of chat. I see a woman I vaguely know and we smile at each other. She's thin as a rake and dressed head-to-toe in trendy and expensive lululemon gear. I know she's done nothing wrong, but the sight of her instantly makes me feel daggy and uncomfortable.

This is not my scene, I tell myself to try to flip my insecure feelings around so that I feel cocky and aloof about the whole experience. (This is a technique that has worked for me before.)

We head to the back of the room, lay our mats out and take off our jackets and shoes—moving fast, because the instructor at the front has already started talking and it looks like she wants everything quiet. She's telling us to sit with our legs straight out in front of us and to stretch over and touch our toes. I do that without too much trouble. Then she has us move our arms out to the side and do some twists. I do them. It's been a long time since I tried to twist or bend my body in any significant way and I feel pretty stiff, but I must admit it feels kind of good to be trying.

After a while we stand up and start doing sun salutations. Everyone is silently following the instructions and I'm sure they all know exactly what they're doing, but I'm struggling to follow what the instructor is saying so I keep looking at everyone else to copy their moves. I struggle through, trying to follow along as best I can (planks are hell; child's poses are lovely), but for the most part my inner dialogue is chattering away telling me how much I hate yoga and how unfit and inflexible I am and how everyone else in the room is perfectly in the yoga zone and I am not.

Twenty minutes in (I know this because I am constantly checking the clock), I'm upside down in a downward dog with my arms shaking from the effort of holding my body in this unfamiliar pose. From this unfortunate position it becomes abundantly clear that not only is my upper-body strength nearly non-existent, but also I made a massive error with my clothing choice. The T-shirt I have on is so baggy it has flopped down and is covering my face, hindering my breathing and completely exposing my tummy and bra—this is *not* what I wanted to happen! I have to twist my head to the side to free my mouth from the material and in doing so catch sight of my friend downward-dogging next to me. She glances over, we lock eyes, and from her upside-down position she slowly stage-whispers to me, 'Don't queef.' I get the giggles, which causes my arms to collapse and my body to fall heavily on my mat. Embarrassing!

Towards the end of the class (eighteen minutes to go and counting) the instructor tells us all to find a spot around the edge of the room because we're going to do headstands, using the wall for support. Nooooooo! This is my worst nightmare! I start whispering to my friend about how much I dislike headstands and the instructor, who is still explaining how to get into the pose, does a little 'Shhh' in my direction, which puts me right back into the old class I hated so much.

Yoga sucks, I tell myself firmly, over and over.

Luckily, most people in the class struggle with the headstands, so the instructor says we're done now and it's time for the nice, chilled-out, lying-down-and-breathing-deeply ending of the class (which is apparently charmingly called the 'corpse pose').

I lie still like a dead person and the instructor talks us through a relaxation and I don't really listen because I'm too busy thinking about stuff, but it's nice to be lying down.

And then it's over. For good, as far as I'm concerned. Sadly, as much as I want to boost the contents of my toolbox with a regular yoga practice and relish it as much as others do, I don't think it's going to happen. On the plus side at least there was no unwanted air in unwanted places for me tonight.

MY TOOLBOX

Recovery community

Sober treats

~~Yoga~~

Mindfulness

As I'm gathering my things together, Ms Lululemon comes over to say hi and asks me how I found the class—she's obviously a regular. I feel bad about judging her as snooty when in reality she's very friendly and lovely. (It's not her fault she's slim and groomed or that I have major hang-ups.) We have a quick chat and I admit to her that I don't feel very comfortable doing yoga, that it seems a bit serious or something, and it's not really my thing.

'There's another teacher who takes a different class here in the smaller room up the back on a Tuesday night,' she says. 'Apparently quite a different vibe. You could try that one?'

'Oh, OK. Maybe I'll do that,' I mumble.

'Lovely to see you, anyway!' Ms Lululemon waves goodbye

and floats out of the door like a butterfly. I buffalo-stomp out behind her with the friend I came with.

'Well?' my friend asks. 'What did you think?'

'Meh. It was fine, I suppose. Not too tiring, but I'd love to be a bit stronger and more flexible.'

'Same,' she says. 'I'm sure it will happen if we come more often. But isn't it great that we're not at home right now putting the kids to bed!'

I hadn't thought of that. She's right! While I've been hanging upside down staring at my boobs, Corin's been at home dealing with the kids. Bonus!

I tell her what Ms Lululemon said about the Tuesday-night class.

'Maybe we should try it?' my friend says and although every fibre of my being is screaming *No!* there's obviously one little rogue fibre that doesn't yet want to give up because I find myself uttering the words, 'OK. One last shot. Tuesday night at the start of next term.'

'Deal.'

It's a nice, quiet house that I return to five minutes later. The kids are in bed, the kitchen is tidy and Corin has the kettle on. I could get used to this.

I make us each a cup of tea and, because I'm feeling good about having just done something healthy, I reward myself with some chocolate. Lots of chocolate, actually. OK, I'll be honest:

I detoured to the store on my way home from the yoga class and bought chocolate. I felt like I deserved it after putting myself through downward-dog hell. There goes my broken reward system for you.

Bingo! The reward systems in my brain are totally faulty

It's perhaps no surprise that the next morning any positive feelings I had from going to a yoga class have been squashed by guilt over my chocolate binge. This is exactly how I used to wake up after a booze binge—feeling emotionally low, weak and disappointed in myself. Why did I feel the need to reward myself with something that makes me feel bad about myself? Sure, in the moment, sugar is delicious, but the emotional after-effects and self-loathing are foul. In the tough early days of sobriety, I could get away with having sweet things as one of my sober treats, but now that wine is not on my radar at all any more I can hardly call a block of white chocolate on the sofa at night a sober treat. It's a dysfunctional crutch that is dragging me down—as evidenced by my sugar hangover this morning.

My sugar habit is no casual thing. I use sugar and highly processed carbs in exactly the same way I used to use booze. In times of extreme emotion, I use them to reward, numb, punish, fill the gap, avoid the silence ... The list goes on. And unfortunately, as with alcohol, I have no ability to moderate the damn stuff. I'm an all-or-nothing gal. If I open a packet of biscuits, I'll eat seven. If I'm in a funk, I'll finish all the cooking chocolate in the house. If there is nothing else available, I'll have a tiny bowl of cereal heaped with three huge spoonfuls of white sugar. Dysfunctional to the max.

Unfortunately (or fortunately, depending on your view-point), in my seemingly inexhaustible mission to fix myself I am no longer able to ignore the ugly truth about my out-of-control sugar habit. It probably doesn't help (or does help, depending on your viewpoint) that the internet is swimming with news and views about the stuff. Every day in my Facebook feed, countless articles claiming to reveal the nasty truth about sugar are shared (alongside countless delicious-looking recipes for cakes and slices—Facebook has a twisted split personality). Sugar is the new tobacco. The world has gone utterly mad about the stuff. You're either living sugar free and raving about how great you feel, or you're not living sugar free and feeling permanently guilty, or you're gleefully consuming it without a care in the world. Or, if you're me, you flick incessantly between all three of these realities.

I have had phases when I've been able to cut out the stuff and felt physically and emotionally great, but permanently deprived. I've had phases when I've been eating it and not caring what anyone thinks, but that never lasts; soon my intake increases and I enter the phase when I'm going crazy for the stuff and constantly feeling guilty and miserable. Usually this phase goes on until I hit a sugar rock-bottom and cut it out again and return to the abstinence phase.

I have no idea how to stop this cravings–binging–self-loathing cycle. With alcohol, my solution was clean-cut: take the substance away completely and learn how to live without it. It's not so easy to be that rigid with sugar, as it's every-bloody-where, and before I know it I'm having a little piece of cake at someone's house and the cravings start again. It grabs hold of me and off I go on the cycle of joy and pain.

Talking to my friends and family about this doesn't help. Half of them tell me not to worry about it, that I can't be perfect, and that everyone deserves treats every now and then. This just gives my addict's brain permission to keep indulging (and my indulgences always end up being extreme). The other half of them say, 'Just have a little bit every now and then,' forgetting that my moderation button was broken at birth. If only it were as simple as just having a little bit every now and then. How easy life would be. This is not my reality.

Right now, in my sugar-hangover funk, I decide that knowledge is the golden ticket that will set me free. I resolve to spend the morning researching and informing myself about the perils of sugar and exactly what it does to my body and how it impacts on my mind. The library books I have reserved on the subject have come in, so I sit myself down with them and a mug of chai tea. I decide to type up everything I learn as a blog post on Living Sober so it will qualify as work as well.

One of the books is called *The Mood Cure* by Julia Ross. It was recommended to me by a blog reader (I'm always going on about my sugar issue on my blog). Julia cuts to the chase, calling sugar one of the most addictive substances on the planet. She says chocolate and other sugary things, and baked foods (anything made from wheat or white flour), can all raise endorphin levels dramatically and therefore, according to Julia, they have 'drug-like effects on your brain's pleasure sites'. Well, there you go. It's no bloody surprise I'm hooked on sugar and highly processed carbs. Julia's book is very information dense and has loads of useful tips in it.

Sarah Wilson's book *I Quit Sugar* (which I actually bought from my local bookstore when I was feeling motivated to be healthy one day) is mostly recipes (that I haven't used) but also includes a lot of information. Sarah echoes Julia on the 'sugar is evil and addictive' front, also describing it as acting like a drug in your brain.

Now I'm curious about the reward systems in my brain. What are those? I decide to take a look at what Dr Libby Weaver has to say on the subject. She's a biochemist and women's health guru with tons of books out. I have been to see her talk in person as well (she's a powerhouse), and have heard her describe how sugar impacts on the brain by releasing dopamine. I'm pretty sure dopamine is a danger chemical for addicts like me, and, sure enough, Dr Libby confirms it.

> When dopamine is low you tend to feel flat. When levels surge it can lead to elation and anything that gives us a lift in mood can become addictive, if we have no other ways to access these uplifted feelings.

Clearly, from an early age I've struggled to access uplifting feelings without some sort of help (hello, alcohol; hello, sugar), and as a result the reward systems in my brain are totally wonky. For years I've been hard-wiring the neural pathways that go desire–action–reward. No wonder I can't resist that block of white chocolate or that fifth piece of shortbread. I need to find ways to access uplifted feelings naturally. Good thing I'm on a mission to do just that . . .

As I read up about sugar, I discover that apparently there's another problem with it: not only does it mess with my brain's pleasure receptors, but my body doesn't register it the same way as other foods so it doesn't fill me up. As Sarah Wilson explains, we 'don't have a natural off-switch for sugar'. When we eat sugar, she says, our bodies don't notice it like it would, say, a meat pie.

OK. So sugar might not have the same obvious impact on my brain that booze does—I don't feel a sugar rush in the same way as I feel drunk—but it clearly does have an impact somewhere deep in my physicality, and certainly on the neurotransmitters in my brain. The more sugary crap I eat, the more I crave it. If I'm in a funk or a low place in my life, I crave it even more.

This sugar research has been enlightening, and after an hour or two spent typing my findings into a blog post for the Living Sober community (many of whom struggle like I do with sugar—no surprises there) I feel a renewed sense of strength and determination. Maybe I'll finally kick this nasty habit to the curb once and for all, and be able to add 'Sugar-free diet' to my toolbox. Here's hoping this newfound information will help me quit the habit and set me free!

(Spoiler alert: it doesn't.)

Chapter 8

I just fall back into moving around my life in the same old way that I always have—like a busy, floating, munching head

It would appear that more information does not always equal changed habits for me. I do manage to pull back on my sugar intake for a while, but it doesn't last. Old thinking habits are even harder to change. Mum comes to stay for a few days, and I slip back into my habit of getting caught up in my thoughts. I'm extra busy trying to make sure her visit runs smoothly and I forget about (or can't be bothered) trying to ground myself by consciously and mindfully focusing on the things around me.

Why would I pause in the shower to notice the feeling of the warm water on my back when I need to plan what meals I'm going to cook that day? How can I clear my mind to focus on my hands working in the soap suds in the kitchen sink when I've got Mum standing at the bench chatting to me? And how on earth can I possibly find a corner to sit in quietly with my eyes closed, focusing on my breath, without others in the house wondering where I've gone or—shock horror!—catching me in the act and asking what the hell I'm doing? They'd think I was a bloody nutter!

I'm pretty convinced I was a bit crap at the sit-down stuff anyway. Don't think I was doing it right. Don't think it gave me any real benefit. It was a bit boring.

After a busy four days, Mum leaves and I'm super tired from trying to be the perfect hostess. No time to rest, though: I've got lots of online sites to keep updated, talks to practise and three sons to feed and run around after. I get back into thinking, planning, worrying, processing, analysing, preparing ... You name it, I'm doing it. I've got an endless internal narrative going on about all the usual stuff in my life—nothing terribly awful or deeply fascinating, but enough to keep me preoccupied, self-absorbed and permanently on edge. Certainly enough to stop me from being the super chilled-out, uber-grounded, Zen housewife I was hoping to become.

I can see what I'm doing. I notice that I'm repeating thought patterns over and over, but I don't take any steps to stop it. I just fall back into moving around my life in the same old way that I always have—like a busy, floating, munching head.

Nothing mindful that I've tried so far has become a habit or really made a difference. Maybe mindfulness and all this trying-to-let-go-of-thoughts business is just too hard for a pleb like me? Gratitude, on the other hand—maybe that's a practice I can nail.

The only reason I'm even still considering gratitude is because people won't stop tweeting about it. I still don't have any idea how to put it into practice, though. I've had a vague idea that I could start each day by thinking of something I'm grateful for before I get out of bed, but that never happens.

I've also wondered about using the time I spend waiting for the traffic lights to change as a trigger to think grateful thoughts, but I never do. (I've also heard it suggested that waiting for the traffic lights to change is a good time to practise pelvic-floor exercises, but I don't ever do them either.)

I have no good ideas for how to incorporate a gratitude practice into my life. None, that is, until my (potential) bestie Elizabeth Gilbert pops up on Facebook with one that seems like it could actually work.

I'm scrolling mindlessly through my news feed, looking at the boring holiday snaps of a random person I met at a barbecue once and watching a hilarious video of a dad demonstrating how to hold a baby, when me ol' mate Liz pops up with a photograph of a large, fancy jar filled with bits of folded-up paper.

Underneath the photo she has written the caption: *This photo is my most recent Jar of Happiness, loyally filled with little scraps of old bills and junk mail, with the best moment of each day scrawled on the back.*

I like this Jar of Happiness! I want one. I think it's the same concept as gratitude—things you are happy about are also things you are grateful for, aren't they?

I get rather excited and immediately go in search of a jar, but I can only find one that smells like gherkins in the back of the kitchen cupboard. It's not very fancy and just won't do.

I scrounge around the house for a while longer before stumbling across a nest of three little bowls in the back of my wardrobe. They were a gift from my sister ages ago; I think she bought them from Trade Aid or someplace. They're woven from recycled paper or plastic—something eco-friendly anyway—and I've never known what the hell to do with them. Well, why not make one of them into a Happiness Bowl? I can be environmentally friendly *and* boost my toolbox at the same time!

MY TOOLBOX

Recovery community

Sober treats

Mindfulness

Gratitude practice (Happiness Bowl)

I put my new Happiness Bowl on the shelf by my computer and get a piece of paper to write down something I'm grateful for. I think for a bit, then write: *I am grateful for my very strong hands, which serve me so well.* Then I fold up the piece of paper, pop it into my bowl, sit back and feel ... well ... nothing much, to be honest. My world doesn't dramatically shift on its axis. I'm not miraculously cured of my mental ills. But it's not a horrible thing to do, either.

The next day I remember to find another scrap of paper and on it I scrawl: *I am grateful for my reading glasses.* It's true. I am. Not sure I'd be able to spend so much time staring at my phone if they weren't there to improve my eyesight. The next day I write: *I am grateful that we are financially stable.* That's a good one, because I don't often remember to be grateful for that and I should be, because not everyone is. It's quite nice to be thinking of something that I usually take for granted. Maybe that's the point of the exercise?

The next day I forget to write anything because, you know, life and all that.

I manage one the next day, though: *I am grateful for my amazing husband.* That feels good (and imagining how nice he'd think I was if he discovered the note feels even better). I can see that it's a good thing to be doing—coming up with something positive to write every day—but I'm still not convinced that it's going to have any real impact on my day-to-day life. It's certainly not dramatic enough for me to shout it from the rooftops or anything. And, unfortunately, it's not enough to stop the noise in my head. Things are still very busy up there. Little energy puffs are flying around with gay abandon and I'm letting them dominate my reality. My thoughts are gospel, and therefore a Zen housewife I ain't. I'm much the same as I was before this new project to fix my life began, except that now, on top of everything else, I have a feeling of failure that stems from the awareness that I haven't been able to make any huge headway (other than successfully letting go of the internal battle I was having with an oblivious mum).

I'm about to mentally cross mindfulness off my list of tools when I get an email notification that the last of my reserved library books has arrived at the local branch and is ready to be collected. En route to pick the boys up from school, I drive past the library to grab it. When I get to school there's still half an hour left before the bell rings. Usually I doodle around on my phone while I wait, but today I take a look at my new library book instead.

All I know is that he has one of the grooviest surnames I've ever heard

It's just a little thing: a white paperback with an image of a messed-up ball of string on the front. The title is *Mindfulness: An eight-week plan for finding peace in a frantic world*. I notice it's written by two people—Mark Williams and Danny Penman. On the back cover it says: 'The book offers simple and straightforward forms of mindfulness meditation that can be done by anyone. You'll be surprised by how quickly these techniques will have you enjoying life again.'

That sounds really good, Mark and Danny. And I like the sound of an eight-week plan. Something concrete to follow, rather than me stumbling through my own self-directed, haphazard plan. Maybe I just need Mark and Danny to be my guides for a few weeks?

I open to the foreword, which has been written by some dude with the coolest surname in the world—Mr Kabat-Zinn. He writes:

Mindfulness is not merely a good idea: 'Oh yes, I will just be more present in my life, and less judgmental, and everything

111

will be better. Why didn't that occur to me before?' Such ideas are at best fleeting and hardly ever gain sustained traction. While it might very well be a good idea to be more present and less judgmental, you won't get very far with the idea alone. In fact, that thought might just make you feel more inadequate or out of control.

Yes! This is me right now to a tee. I *do* feel terribly inadequate about my failed attempts to improve myself with mindfulness.

I find out later that Jon Kabat-Zinn is a total legend in the world of mindfulness and meditation. He's a Professor of Medicine Emeritus at the University of Massachusetts Medical School, where he founded the Center for Mindfulness in Medicine, Health Care, and Society. He's carried out numerous scientific studies on the benefits of mindfulness, has written many bestselling books, and is highly sought after to speak on the subject. He's credited with bringing mindfulness and meditation out of the realm of hippies and into mainstream awareness. Of course, I'm not aware of any of this as I sit in my car; all I know is that he has one of the grooviest surnames I've ever heard. I read on: 'To be effective, mindfulness requires an embodied engagement on the part of anyone hoping to derive some benefit from it. Mindfulness is a practice.'

Embodied engagement. A practice. In other words, it's something that I have to stay actively engaged with and do regularly. I know that this is much easier said than done.

I look at my watch—three minutes till the bell goes. I look out of the window and see parents heading into the school. I look up at the sky and take a deep breath.

I don't want to give up on this. I don't want to give up on the goal I set for myself all those weeks ago. I really don't. A Happiness Bowl, while fun, isn't going to fix my internal angst. I look back down at the little paperback in my hands and another line from Mr Cool-Surname catches my eye. He tells me that, over time, mindfulness will improve my mood, levels of happiness and overall feelings of wellbeing.

I feel a sort of desperate yearning. I so want this. I want to achieve a much more sustainable measure of calm inside my head. I want to not stress about the little things. I want to be open and compassionate to all the people I come across—even the tricky ones. I want to parent mindfully and raise my three gorgeous, complicated sons as best I can.

I clasp the book tightly to my chest and make a pledge to myself. I am going to hitch my wagon to Danny and Mark and follow their eight-week plan to the letter. Starting now! Or ...

Immediately I begin coming up with excuses for why now is not a good time to start. I think about the weeks ahead. I'm away travelling next week to give my talks, and we're all going on holiday for a week over Easter. Maybe I should put it off until I've got a clear eight weeks in front of me with no distractions?

The school bell has gone and kids are pouring out through the gate. I can see my sons approaching the car, bags dragging and mouths moving. Pretty soon my space will become noisy and chaotic.

No. Bugger it. I want to do this now.

There will always be a reason not to start. The time is now. Tomorrow the eight-week plan begins.

No more of that sitting cross-legged on the floor malarkey for me

The next morning, I get out of bed before anyone is up and head down to the study, ready to start my eight-week plan. I read the introduction to the book while drinking my tea the night before, so I know a little about what the plan is going to have me do. Among other things, I'm going to have to listen to some short audio tracks that Danny and Mark have made available online.

Once I'm set up in the study (lights on, door shut), I use the iPad to navigate to the web page where they've stored their audio tracks. I hit the green DOWNLOAD button next to the one labelled MEDITATION ONE. Immediately I get a pop-up message saying Safari is unable to download this file. Well, thanks a bunch, Safari. Don't you know I'm on a mission to change my life here?

I try hitting the little blue arrow next to MEDITATION ONE and up pops a little audio-player screen. I hit PLAY and it starts. Success! A nice man with an English accent (Danny? Mark?) starts telling me how I should be sitting. It's so great hearing his voice—he sounds very smooth and calm and kind.

He tells me that I can sit on a chair if I like with my feet flat on the floor and uncrossed. Thank goodness I don't have to put myself back into a position I haven't been comfortable in since the 1970s. No more of that sitting cross-legged on the floor malarkey for me.

Before I have a chance to get into much more of the audio I hear a little boy coming up the stairs. He does a noisy wee in the toilet (why do they never shut the door?), then thumps down the hallway and starts talking loudly to Corin.

Still with my eyes shut, I try to block out their chatter and remain focused on the nice English man talking. But now there's something wrong with the iPad's audio player. The audio keeps getting stuck and jumping back a few seconds, and stopping, then jumping back again. This is not meditative; it's frustrating as all hell! Bugger this. I give up and get on with the morning—in, I'm ashamed to admit, a rather grumpy fashion. I'm so sick of these things not working properly.

It's a bad start.

But I'm determined, and later that afternoon I get a chance to try again before school pick-up. This time I find the online tracks using my phone and for some reason the audio player on this device works OK. I sit on a chair in the kitchen and listen to the nice, kind-sounding English man (Danny? Mark?) guide me through a track that is all about focusing on my breath and my body. Of course my mind wanders like buggery the entire time—I seem to have the attention span of a gnat—but it's nice to have someone guiding me, rather than having to try to force myself to focus on my breath. Whoever it is on the track keeps telling me to 'gently escort my thoughts back to the breath'. I start to wonder why the breath is such a magical thing; I'm always being told to focus on it. What's so special about the breath?

The audio ends after what seems like forever, but it actually only took eight minutes. Very doable.

I then decide I'm going to do something else that's described in the book: a raisin meditation. Yes, a raisin meditation. It's hilarious! Basically, I'm supposed to get a raisin and then take a very, very, verrrrrrry long time to ponder and eat it. Every step along the way with this raisin—holding it, seeing it, touching it, smelling it, placing it in my mouth, chewing it, swallowing it, noticing the after-effects—has to be done for a good 30 seconds, and then I have to write down anything I noticed while doing it all.

I have never even looked at a raisin for 30 seconds, let alone chewed on a raisin for 30 seconds.

Chapter 9

Quite frankly, I don't think I've ever thought about my breath so much in my life!

First I sit the raisin on my palm and just look at it. Then I feel it between my fingers. Then I lift it up to my nose and sniff it a bunch. Then I put it in my mouth, bite it and swallow it, and finally I get a notebook and write in it: *Constantly analysed what I was being asked to do rather than the raisin itself. Mind wandered. Planned how I was going to write about it.* (One of the perils of being a blogger—constantly planning how you are going to write about things you are experiencing.)

After my detailed raisin exploration, I read a bit more of

Mark and Danny's book. It's very easy to follow and there's a ton of great information nestled among the basic instructions for the eight-week plan. I learn that Mark is the kind-sounding man on the audio tracks, and he's the mindfulness guru—a professor of clinical psychology, no less. Danny is the journalist and writer of the pair, although he's also a bit of a mindfulness guru and has a PhD.

Later that evening, while Corin is putting the boys to bed, I try to listen again to the audio track. It's only eight minutes, and I figure for sure Corin will take that long to tuck the boys in and settle them down. I can have it done before he comes back upstairs. But after only two minutes, I hear him stomping his way up the stairs, so I quickly turn it off so that he doesn't see what I'm doing. I'm going to have to get over my embarrassment (and my die-hard belief that meditation is somehow ridiculous and only for hippies) and tell him what I'm doing so that he doesn't come near me for the allotted time. Or I could just shut the study door.

I remember to add a quick note to my Happiness Bowl before I go to bed: *I am very grateful to have lovely parents, who are kind and caring and warm and giving.*

As the week goes on I faithfully follow the plan and keep listening to the audios regularly. Having a set structure to follow is really working for me and I fall slowly in love with Mark and his calm voice. I also remember to do a gratitude note most days.

I start to feel as though Mark is my special friend and personal mindfulness tutor, and that he is talking directly to me and me alone. I even stalk him online and seek out YouTube videos of him delivering talks at various places. He is the most kind-looking man, with a grey beard and smiley eyes, and he's so clever!

My mind wanders every time I listen to his audio, but he keeps telling me not to judge it for doing so and to simply notice I've gone off on some mental tangent or other and bring my attention back to the breath. Honestly, my attention stays on the breath for only the briefest of moments before my mind wanders again. And then I bring it back to the breath. And then it wanders. And then I bring it back to the breath.

Quite frankly, I don't think I've ever thought about my breath so much in my life! I mean, why would you? It hasn't required any attention from me. It's just something that I do over and over without ever thinking about it. Much like how my skin regenerates without me noticing, my lungs breathe of their own accord. It's quite weird to suddenly be paying attention to this action my body does around 20,000 times a day.

On the audio track—which I have listened to over and over by now—the last line Mark delivers is: 'And, remembering that the breath is always available to you, to help bring you back into the present moment, when you find your mind scattered and dispersed by the rush and busyness of your life. Always here, as an anchor deep within you, as a place of stillness, and peace.'

I love this message about the breath being an anchor, a place of stillness and peace. I feel very clever for having figured out why the breath gets so much attention in mindfulness: it's because it's always there, so it's a handy, readily available tool to take the focus away from the energy puffs forming an endless narrative inside my head.

Months later, at a mindfulness workshop, I hear even more reasons why the breath is so powerful and important. I'm told it's a brilliant window into our inner world and a great source of information about how we are doing at any particular time— for example, think of how a shallow breath of terror or a long deep sigh of melancholy communicates what you are feeling. When pausing to focus on your breath, you might notice that it's incredibly shallow and really fast or maybe it's slow and deep. I learn that tuning in to how you are breathing can help you tune in to your current state of mind—it can be like a flashlight on your inner world.

I'm also told that the breath has a naturally soothing element to it, much like listening to the coming and going of gentle ocean waves or watching clouds float calmly by. If we slow our breath down and focus on it, then it can soothe us dramatically.

The point is also made that the breath connects us to nature and the outside world. Each inhalation of oxygen brings the outside world in, while each exhalation of carbon dioxide sends the inside world out. Apparently having this understanding can particularly help you to break up any sense of isolation—you are reminded that you are not alone, you are a part of a much bigger, interconnected world. I especially love this idea!

The workshop also touches on the notion that most of us tend to think of the breath as something incredibly boring (yep), but if you pause for a moment and imagine not being able to do it then it suddenly becomes far from boring. It's vital.

Right now, listening to Mark, I'm just beginning to tap into the power of my breath, and this is having a slightly positive impact on my state of mind. I have to be honest and use the word 'slightly' because the impact is incredibly subtle. There are no dramatic changes to the way that I'm living, but if I take a moment I do notice that, even if it's only for a short time each day, I am spending less time caught up in fraught thinking loops in my head. I am also slightly less inclined to smear ten crackers with butter and jam at four in the afternoon. I wouldn't say it's an earth-shattering change, but it's a change nonetheless.

Blocking out everything in your head kind of feels like telling normal life to go shove it

Unfortunately, it's not enough to stop me getting insomnia. Tossing and turning in bed for hours in the middle of the night is not a very Zen thing to do but, despite my (and Mark's) best efforts, my brain is still wired to get lost in thinking patterns. I try desperately to calm my thoughts and ground myself in my body (use the breath, use the breath) but in the darkness my mind zings around in a million directions. I'm just not that good at mindfulness yet.

It probably doesn't help that I lie in bed surfing the internet for an hour or so every night before attempting to sleep, or that the iPad sits on my bedside table all night long (like an alluring portal to a world of stimulation and fun). As I toss and turn, I think about my blocked ear, about the talks I'm giving next week, about my work, about some other tricky interpersonal stuff that is going on . . . I just go around and around thinking, thinking, thinking. It's been a while since I've had sleepless nights like this (I used to get them all the time when boozing), so on top of all my other worries is my concern about how exhausted I'm going to be in the morning.

Do mindfulness gurus get insomnia? I'd love to know because, bloody hell, I'm finding it really hard to stay all Zen and calm when life keeps getting in the way. *Why does tricky stuff keep happening to me?* I think as I roll around, trying to get comfortable. Woe is me with my busy, complicated life (toss, turn). I ruminate over emails (toss, turn). I speculate over family members' actions (toss, turn).

Being a human is bloody hard work, I surmise right before

I finally fall into a broken sleep, only for the alarm to go off an hour later (I hate that).

This bout of insomnia leaves me feeling like rat shit. I'm super tired and wired but, rather than slump into a pit of wallowing despair, I force myself to keep doing the mindful tasks as instructed by Danny and Mark. Having their plan to follow is good—it's giving me something to focus on, which I sorely need. I can't afford to collapse in a tired, teary heap.

One of the things they're still getting me to do is sit and focus on a bloody raisin every day. It has been proving rather an interesting exercise, actually. After my first day's fail, when I hardly thought about the raisin at all (and thought about thinking about the raisin instead, if that makes sense), I've got a bit more connected with this tiny, wrinkled brown thing.

The second time I did the raisin meditation, I wrote in my notebook afterwards: *Mind wandered. Tried not to judge. Raisin felt much bigger in my mouth than when it was in my hand— some grooves felt really deep under my tongue.*

The next day, I noted: *Mind wandered. Takes a while to clear the raisin out of my mouth. Yummy.*

And then the next day, this: *Mind wandered. Thought about what the raisin had been before it became a raisin and who looked after it.*

It's amazing what you can focus on when you give yourself the time and space to do it. It crosses my mind that I could be similarly slow and considered with sweet or starchy treat foods. Maybe that would stop me gobbling them when the urge hits? But I somehow conveniently forget to ever do that.

As the first week draws to a close and I get some better sleep patterns back, I'm feeling pretty good at having mostly stuck to Danny and Mark's plan. I haven't managed to do the raisin meditation seven times as I should have (probably more like four), but I have been listening to their audio track regularly, and I've done the other activities as instructed—things like changing the chair I sit in at dinner—and that has been interesting. I am also discovering how much my mind wanders during every single routine task I do. It's hard to focus only on brushing your teeth while you are busy brushing them!

But I do believe this increased emphasis on mindfulness has cemented the practice as a real tool in my toolbox. Despite my recent bout of insomnia, I've been feeling fairly calm overall, not too lost in thought or wound up in my own head. I am definitely much more aware of staying in the moment, really listening to my kids when they talk, noticing lots of things around me visually, and the sensations beneath my feet and in my hands. I spend a lot of time driving my three boys to school and various activities, so I'm using that time to try to stay super mindful of the feel of the car as I grip the steering wheel. And of the sun as it hits the windscreen. And of the horizon line around my city. It's good that I'm really settling into my mindfulness practice, because my gratitude practice has died a sudden death. I've completely stopped putting pieces of paper into my Happiness Bowl. Sorry, Liz.

MY TOOLBOX

Recovery community

Sober treats

Mindfulness

~~Gratitude practice (Happiness Bowl)~~

As it turns out, the mindfulness stuff is quite fun, because it is taking me away from what I'm normally used to doing. Switching off and peace-ing out in my brain for a while is such a great concept. In fact, I've started getting this crazy idea that mindfulness is somehow rebellious and countercultural. Blocking out everything in your head kind of feels like telling normal life to go shove it.

Part of why I used to love alcohol so much was that it felt rebellious. It felt naughty to get sloshed and step outside of normal life for a while. I always felt excited about my reality being shifted and the norm being altered for a while. (And, let's face it, I'm a booze-hound so I also just really liked everything about alcohol, full stop.) But I'm starting to have an inkling of a similar feeling about mindfulness.

It's kind of crazy transgressive to sit with your eyes shut and try to stop your racing brain by just thinking about your breath. It is countercultural to reject the inner dialogue about all the things I normally worry about and instead focus my full attention on some wondrous aspect of nature—which, when I start really focusing in on it, becomes rather spectacular. Thoughts and worries and plans are flying at me every moment, tempting and distracting me, so to stop and deflect them feels rebellious. The rebel in me loves the slightly naughty feeling I get from rejecting all the trivial thoughts that I would have been paying attention to before. I love this subtle but actually quite huge change in my thinking. Why worry about so many little things just because I always have? Just because society says I should? Phooey to that! And especially in this day and age, when the internet is ever-present on our devices, sucking us in to its endless, magical charms (or its soul-sucking evil pit, depending on your point of view). Resisting the internet's allures to instead spend time alone focusing on your breath feels rebellious in the extreme. It's fun to stop all the thinking and web-surfing and just 'be' a breathing human being.

And, I must admit, it's exciting to imagine a time when I might experience a shift in consciousness—a heightened awareness like that which some of the authors I have read describe. I hope that will happen soon!

I'm not sure that mindfulness and social media mix at all well

It doesn't. Instead, I get mega-edgy because it's time to head away on my speaking trip. It's a rare occurrence for me to leave the house overnight, let alone for two nights, so I have a lot to organise. I have to write lists for Corin of what is happening with the boys while I'm gone. I have to liaise with other parents to organise pick-ups and drop-offs. I have to fill the fridge and freezer with foods that will be eaten without any fuss (hopefully). I have to pack my bags and prepare myself mentally to go on show as a shining example of a sober superstar (ha ha). And of course I have to get myself ready to continue with my mindfulness plan while I'm away.

On the eve of my departure, while Corin is tucking the boys into bed, I sit myself down in the study (with the door closed this time—I have learned my lesson!) and read through Danny and Mark's instructions for the week ahead. Apparently I'm now going to be learning how to pay mindful attention to my body.

They write a lot about the body–mind connection, and it's great reading. Bottom line is that our bodies powerfully influence our thoughts. Our bodies are acutely sensitive to the finest flickering of emotion in our minds, and the state of our bodies can significantly affect the judgements we make from moment to moment. Simply altering our relationship to our bodies can profoundly improve our lives.

Well, who knew?

This is *very* interesting to me, because I have always known that I am quite disconnected from my body—that 'floating head' or 'living from the shoulders up' syndrome that I have experienced. I don't feel very in touch with my physical self in a day-to-day way at all, and I know that my twenty-plus years of drinking has left me quite numb to not just my emotions but also to my physical self. My body has always just been there doing its thing, sometimes hurting or causing me grief but mostly just acting as it should. As a result of this non-attention, I've never felt very grounded in my body—or at least not until recently, when I started thinking about my breath regularly for the first time ever, did a yoga class, and began trying to do body-scans. As unusual as it has been for me to think about my breath, it has been even more of a foreign concept to focus my attention on my feet or knees for a sustained period of time in order to notice any sensations there.

I decide to listen to the next guided track right now in the study, so I set myself up in a comfy spot on the floor—with my head on a cushion and a blanket over me—and hit play. Mark's lovely voice starts talking, telling me to notice the sense of my body as a whole. Then he says I have to remind myself that I'm not trying to get anywhere in particular, nor am I striving to achieve any special state.

No, Mark, you're wrong. I *am* trying to achieve a special state. I *am* waiting for the magical moment that others have described. I want Elizabeth Gilbert's 'intense, vibrating, awed silence'. I want Dan Harris's 'amazing', 'thrilling' and 'exhilarating' mental breakthrough. *It's gotta be round the corner*, I tell myself, and I get so caught up imagining the lovely state of nirvana I will one day achieve, along with a bunch of other inane thoughts, that I forget to listen to Mark's body-scan and only tune back in when he is wrapping things up. Whoops-a-daisy!

Undeterred by my failed body-scan, I head away the next day determined to be mindful for the duration of my trip. I mindfully talk to the taxi driver on the way to the airport (trying to really listen to him and notice the look and feel of his car). I mindfully check in for my flight (really noticing the process and marvelling at the efficiency of the airline's systems). I mindfully buy myself a mindless women's magazine at the airport bookstore (taking time to survey the endless rows of mags and ponder the craziness of this intensely glossy industry). I spot my own memoir, *Mrs D Is Going Without*, on the shelf and try to surreptitiously take a photo of it on my phone before sharing it to Instagram (#proud). I don't manage to stay very mindful (or surreptitious) through this self-congratulatory photo-taking-and-uploading process, and I get a bit lost mindlessly scrolling through other people's photos on Instagram for a while (*Oh, look, a cat on a table!*). I'm not sure that mindfulness and social media mix at all well.

I intend to mindfully drink my coffee as I wait for my flight, but I forget and instead manage to gulp my way through most of it before remembering that for one of my Week Two tasks I'm supposed to savour every aspect of my hot drinks (#fail).

I get my mindful mojo back in time for boarding. I mindfully pass through the departure gate (worn carpet, jaded travellers, groomed gate staff), and mindfully walk across the tarmac to the tiny plane that will take me to my destination (painted lines, smelly fumes, cold wind). Being super mindful of this boarding process is actually really great—I feel alive to the experience and rather cool approaching the plane, like I'm a celebrity approaching my private jet. As I climb the stairs into the plane, I'm reminded of the feeling I had when I first went travelling in my early twenties. Everything seems rather exciting all of a sudden!

My excitement is short-lived, however. As I mindfully sit down in my seat (small, cramped) I start to mindfully notice how terrifyingly minuscule this plane is (terrifyingly minuscule, terrifyingly minuscule), and proceed to get very nervous. I can't be anything but mindful of my present-moment experience at this point—this plane is minute! There is only one seat on either side of the aisle. I don't even need to lean to the side to see right through to the cockpit. There is no door on the cockpit. In fact, I don't know that you would even call it a cockpit—it's just a teeny section at the front of a teeny aircraft. It's like we're sitting in a tin can with wings. I can see the pilots pushing buttons and knobs. I can see the windscreen. I can see the windscreen wipers! I can actually look right through the windscreen as though I am in the back seat of a car, looking at the road ahead. This isn't right.

As we taxi down the runway and bump through a rough take-off, I start to mindfully freak out about how small this flying machine is. How on earth does it stay up in the sky? What was that beeping coming from the cockpit just now? There's another beep—a long one. It's still going. What the hell is this long drawn-out beep?!

I don't like being mindful of this flying process at all. I'd far rather be lost in thought about something inane, or even something fraught. I'd rather be having an internal conversation with someone tricky than sitting here, gripping the armrests, feeling terrified about this tiny plane. This is no fun.

I mindfully reach for my mindless women's magazine and deliberately try to distract myself from the present moment by reading up on celebrity gossip. I ignore the indiscriminate beeping noises and force myself to care about Johnny Depp's new young bride called Amber somebody (looks like a keeper). I resist looking out of the front windscreen and instead ponder the speculation that Jennifer Garner and Ben Affleck are set to divorce (no way—they seem so happy). I sip my tiny container of water and wonder whether Kate and William are going to have a boy or a girl sibling for Prince George.

The Royal Family does it for me. I happily go off on a huge mental tangent, pondering what it would be like to grow up as a princess (one of my favourite childhood fantasies) and this carries me through the rest of the nerve-wracking flight.

Chapter 10

My feet are actually a hive of static activity!

A few hours later I'm lying on the bed in my motel room with my shoes off and my eyes closed. I have a couple of free hours before I need to front up at a local cafe and bare my soul to a large group of women. I am listening to Mark.

He tells me to bring my attention down to my breath in my abdomen, and to notice as my abdomen stretches when I breathe in and falls away when I breathe out.

I do this.

He tells me to gather my attention and move it down my body to my feet.

I do this, too.

He tells me to notice what sensations are in both my feet when my attention arrives here. In my toes, the soles of my feet, the heels, the top of my feet.

I concentrate hard on my feet. *There's nothing going on there*, I think.

But then I notice a slight hum of energy, followed by an awareness of the pressure on both heels where they come into contact with the mattress. And there's a very slight itch in the little toe of my right foot. OMG! My feet are actually a hive of static activity!

I carry on like this right round my whole body, really concentrating hard on all the sensations in each body part and connecting with them. For the first time ever, I'm totally immersed in this process. Maybe it's because I'm away from home and there are no distractions. Maybe it's because I'm nervous and don't want to think about the talk I'm about to give. Or maybe it's because my faltering yet determined attempts thus far to get into mindfulness have at last led me towards better concentration.

Whatever the case, as Mark guides me around the parts of my body, I am fully alive and alert to all of them. It feels really good. Calming. And quite intriguing actually. There are loads of subtle yet noticeable sensations in my body. It's significantly more pronounced, this connection that I feel to my body, as I lie on the bed alone in a motel room in a tiny town far from home.

After fifteen minutes of body-scanning, Mark signs off with one final, encouraging message: he tells me to let myself be just as I am, complete and whole, and to rest in my awareness at each moment.

I take a deep breath, sit up and actually say out loud to the empty motel room, 'Amazing.'

It *is* amazing. It's hard to translate this experience into words, but I feel like I have just had a real 'coming home' to my body.

I wouldn't call it a monumental breakthrough or anything— no way. It was far more subtle than that. But it was something new. Something a little bit deep. Something a little bit exciting. And certainly something very grounding. Incredibly grounding, actually.

I feel calm as I shower and get dressed into the 'new' black dress I got for the talk from a second-hand shop. I feel calm as I walk down the road to the cafe where I'm speaking. I feel calm as I chat to the ladies gathered to hear me talk. I feel calm eating my meal. I feel calm as I stand and begin my story. I get totally lost in my story and then I cry when I recount my final night drinking... but I always do that. I feel calm answering the questions at the end. I feel calm as I eat my pudding.

I'm usually pretty relaxed about public speaking, but this evening I feel particularly present and grounded. Is this because I've had a few goes at public speaking already? Or is it because of the mindfulness training I've been doing? It must be the latter, as I notice that I keep pausing during the evening to breathe deeply and centre myself. Maybe the mindfulness training *is* having an effect after all...

As the evening wraps up, I'm chatting to one woman and somehow we get on to the topic of mindfulness. She admits she's been working on learning these techniques as well. Mindfulness really is all the rage, then. Good to know I'm on trend.

I go back to the motel feeling rather proud of myself, and happy that the mindfulness stuff seems to be having an impact. Maybe this is how I'm going to live the rest of my life! Always calm, my mind in the present, not fretting about the energy bubbles and looking fly. (Unfortunately, when I'm sent photos of the event a month or so later I discover my 'new' black dress was transparent and the white bra I'd worn underneath was highly visible. Clearly mindfulness isn't going to fix my tendency to suffer fashion fails.)

Later that evening, after I've eaten my celebratory piece of ginger crunch back in my motel room—blissfully unaware that I've just flashed my underwear to a large group of people—I decide to listen to Mark's body-scan audio again. Unfortunately, I'm so worn out from the evening's activities that I start to nod off towards the end. Whoopsie!

I make up for it by doing the body-scan twice more the next

day, while waiting to give my talk to a different group of ladies. (I also manage to squeeze in some shopping, a manicure and some mindless TV-watching—got to have balance in life!)

My talk on the second night goes well. Different cafe, different group of ladies, equally as successful as the first one. No see-through dress this time, though. Once again, I remember to breathe deeply and ground myself to counter any nerves I feel. Once again, I cry when recounting my final night of drinking. Once again, the topic of mindfulness comes up when I'm mingling with the group afterwards. I'm starting to feel marginally less self-conscious about this mindful mission I'm on. After more celebratory sugar back in my motel room (mindfulness has not yet cured me of my faulty reward switch, which remains firmly set to 'sugar'), I consider the trip to have been a success.

None of this would be happening to me if I'd continued on my boozy path. I'm so, so happy to be sober and spreading the word about the wonders of recovery. It is wonderful to be living in the raw all the time, even if I am still battling to develop new emotional coping mechanisms. I feel infinitely happier and more proud of myself than I ever have. I also feel more authentic, like I'm approaching every situation as the real me, warts and all. It's fantastic.

Another tin can flies me home the following morning (and another mindless magazine helps distract me during the flight), and once I'm safely back home I remain dedicated to the mindful cause. I keep listening to Mark's audio regularly and doing the other things as instructed by the book. Because I'm so in the zone with all this mindful work, I'm finding myself more likely to notice what is actually happening in front of me, rather than what's happening in my head. It's particularly easy to do this when I'm doing boring things, like driving the car (feeling the vibrations of the car beneath my hands on the steering wheel, and noticing nature outside the window), washing the dishes (observing the bubbles in the water), and standing in the shower (feeling the warm water on my back, and noticing the smell of the soap).

Somehow, though, I can't for the life of me remember to pay conscious attention when brushing my teeth or drinking hot drinks! I don't know what it is about these two activities, but I'm always getting to the end of them before I realise I've been completely lost in thought throughout. It's a bummer.

After gulping my way through yet another mug of instant decaf coffee I decide to set myself up to really nail this exercise, once and for all. Right before I'm due to go and pick up the boys from school, I prepare myself a pot of herbal tea and pour some of it into a travel mug with a lid. I then drive to school and park up outside; I've got enough time to spare before the bell goes to properly savour my tea. I'm going to mindfully drink this sucker if it kills me.

I turn the car off, pick up the mug and get started.

Holy shit, this mindfulness stuff really works!

I stare at the mug—this is me using my sense of sight. Staring at the mug. It's a deep-blue plastic with a wide rubber strip around the middle.

I notice the warmth of the liquid coming through the plastic into my hands—this is me using my sense of touch. It's lovely and warm. I think about what a great idea it is to have the rubber strip around the middle of the mug, as it's stopping my hands from getting too hot. I notice that the geometric pattern cut into the rubber is satisfyingly symmetrical (I love symmetry). I slowly rub the tips of my fingers over the pattern and it feels nice. *Mmmmmm.*

Two mums walk past, chatting to one another, and I'm startled out of my reverie. *Holy shit, did they catch me sitting here staring at my mug like it holds the secret to life? Did they see me stroking it lovingly? Hope they don't think I'm stoned or something!*

They move past without glancing my way so I feel safe. Back to the exercise.

I try to employ my sense of sound by listening to the tea but it's resolutely quiet. I jiggle the mug a bit and it makes a tiny sloshing sound, so that's something. Unfortunately, the jiggling also leads to a bit of a spill, which is annoying. Oh well.

Next I raise the mug to my nose and sniff. What a lovely thing to do! This tea smells delicious! Wow! It's a very fancy-pants dragon pearl jasmine tea, and the scent reminds me of the tea at Chinese restaurants. I think about that for a bit (while sniffing) then have a momentary thought about how indulgent I am to buy such fancy and expensive tea (a dollar a bag!), but quickly justify the expense by telling myself it's still a damn sight cheaper than the wine I used to buy in abundance.

More parents are walking past the car. I hunker down in my seat, hoping no one will see me sniffing away madly. I'm proud of myself for really savouring this tea-drinking experience, and, although I do feel a bit silly, I have to admit it *is* rather pleasurable.

Finally I allow myself to sip the tea, letting it sit in my mouth for a moment before swallowing gently. It tastes ah-mazing. Delicate and delicious. I can feel the warmth as it travels down my oesophagus to my stomach—yes, I really am thinking about my oesophagus!

I sip slowly, again and again and again, and it is delectable. I am in tea heaven. Every single drop is savoured until it is all gone. *Yum.*

I can see kids streaming out of the gates, which means the bell has gone. My goodness, where did the time go? I quickly get out of the car to meet my boys, and as I approach the school the whole tea-drinking experience is really staying with me. I feel so warm and satisfied. It's a lovely, contented feeling.

I've just done something seemingly inconsequential yet remarkably gratifying. I'm amazed at how something as simple as making myself concentrate really hard on drinking a mug of tea has made the whole experience heaps more rewarding and pleasurable. It's phenomenal! I do actually feel a little bit like the Zen housewife I'm so desperate to become. Holy shit, this mindfulness stuff really works!

Over the next few days—still listening to Mark regularly and reading the book—it becomes way more habitual for me to stay aware of my present-moment experience, rather than getting caught up in twisted thinking loops. I do still spend a lot of time planning, ruminating, worrying, fantasising, et cetera, but now that I'm waking up to the patterns of my mind I can usually catch myself in the act before it goes on too long. It's almost as though I flick a little mental switch to break myself out of it: I recognise what's happening and I just stop the mind-chatter by forcing myself to notice what my hands are doing or what my eyes can see right in front of me. Such a simple action, yet so powerful.

If I do catch my mind buggering off, getting wound up in thoughts, I'll stop and ask myself, 'What is happening in this moment right now?' And, by golly, I'm starting to realise that 99 per cent of my life is made up of moments that are actually very straightforward and lovely. There's hardly ever anything stressful or negative happening in the moment. Usually I'm just doing something fairly straightforward without any shit going down. It's only my mind that is making me stressed out or anxious by creating little energy puffs in the form of thoughts.

Since I'm much more aware of what my thoughts are telling me, I'm also able to start looking at them with a slightly detached and critical eye. I'm noticing that, particularly when I'm tired or it's a crazy-busy day, my mind will work over-time to create all sorts of unhelpfully negative thoughts, which only serve to wind me up even more. Yet when I'm relaxed or calm (or staring at a mug of tea like it's the holy grail) my mind isn't creating these stressful or unhelpful thoughts at all, and I feel calmer and happier.

I'm starting to realise that it's not so much what these mindfulness exercises are getting me to do (focus on my breath and body, and notice what I can see, hear, smell, feel and taste), as it is what they are *stopping* me from doing (worrying about the future, ruminating over the past, planning, fantasising, carrying out imaginary arguments, getting lost on the internet, gobbling food mindlessly).

I could choose to spend the fifteen minutes waiting for the school bell to go scrolling through Instagram or Twitter, talking on the phone or being lost in thought about something boring going on in my life, but none of these things would serve to chill me out at all. If I choose to spend the time at one with my mug of tea, savouring every single aspect of it, chilled out is exactly what I will be. And this is what I am yearning for!

I have the power to dictate how I spend my free brain time, and the choices I make can have an immense impact on my overall experience of life.

This is a rather mind-blowing revelation, to be honest, and I'm quite buzzed by it all. I feel enlivened! It's much like when I first gave up alcohol and hit the wonderful 'pink cloud' phase of early sobriety, when everything becomes clear. I feel on a high about the radical new perspective on life that exploring mindfulness is giving me.

I've never before questioned the nature of my thoughts, or my allegiance to them. The fact that I'm starting to realise I don't have to be led by what I'm thinking is not only revelatory but also, frankly, life-changing. I'm not exaggerating. I really do feel like my life is being changed by this newfound knowledge that I have about my brain, about the nature of thought, and about the different choices I can make about my mental behavior. It has altered my whole experience of life.

This knowledge is profound! Finally, everything I have been reading and learning about has cemented itself in my brain. I get it. I really get it. This is it! A big life change has occurred. With my newfound knowledge and understanding, I set a bunch of rock-solid habits in place, am cured of all my woes, and everything is perfect for the rest of my life. From here on in, I truly am the perfect example of a Zen housewife.

I am sugar-free and eat only whole foods

Every morning my alarm wakes me at 5.30 am. Soothing sacred chants play gently as I come to consciousness. Before moving a muscle, I lie still and mentally list ten things that I am grateful for. I slide gracefully out of bed and glide down to the study, where I light scented candles and sit comfortably cross-legged on my special meditation cushion ($56.35 from Amazon).

I meditate for an hour. Silently and with no interruptions. I breathe deeply and focus my attention on the air coming into and going out of my body. My legs do not get sore. My attention does not waver. Occasional thoughts arise but not many. I am always firmly in control of my little mental energy puffs and do not let them lead me mindlessly through my days.

I follow up my meditation session with a lovely half hour of advanced yoga. By now I am unbelievably limber and can hold incredibly tricky poses for many minutes (handstands are my favourite).

I remain deeply grounded in my body for the entire day.

I am sugar free and eat only whole foods. I drink only water and herbal tea.

My parenting is at all times calm, attentive, fair, loving and consistent. I handle every tricky person with an open and loving heart.

I practise gratitude and pelvic floor exercises at every red light I come to.

I have set times in the day where I allow myself internet access. I never stray from these times.

I feel at one with nature and its creatures.

I compost, recycle, upcycle and unicycle.

Any free time I have, I listen to mindfulness podcasts, guided meditations and Dharma talks. I smile often, and laugh freely and deeply. I feel calm, truly happy, free from any mental anguish, at peace with the world. Whole.

My toolbox looks like this.

MY TOOLBOX

Recovery community

Sober treats

Mindfulness and meditation

Advanced yoga

Gratitude practice

Marathon running

Sugar-free wholefood diet

Healthy internet habits

Chapter 11

A reality where shit happens and bad moods prevail

If only it were true that from this point on I live as this sort of perfectly perfect human. Never experiencing any fears or worries. Never crying or stuffing my face with muffins when I'm in a funk. Never yelling at my kids or fretting over what other people think of me. Always gliding around on my cloud of joy, sprinkling peace and love wherever I go.

Sadly, this is not how things go.

A week or so after my glorious mug of mindful tea, my mindfulness pink cloud dissipates and dumps me back down on to a steaming pile of reality. A reality where shit happens and bad moods prevail.

It's Sunday night and Corin and I are eating ice cream and watching a TV show about Vikings. I've got Danny and Mark's book in my lap and am trying to read up on what is required of me for the week ahead while also watching leather-clad men fight each other with swords and axes.

I glance down at the book and feel annoyed and over this whole mindfulness thing. I can't be bothered with it. Instead of spending the day observing my thoughts in a detached way, I've been incredibly wound up by them. I've also been locked in a fierce battle of wills with our middle son (the combination of our personalities does not always make for smooth interactions). I'm not in the mood to sit and reflect. I'm annoyed that I have to keep making time every day to sit and listen to a body-scan audio or some such—it's hard to keep finding the time to fit it in. My grateful well also appears to have dried up for good, as I still haven't resumed putting little pieces of paper in my Happiness Bowl. (Sorry again, Liz).

I'm hyper-aware that I'm having these annoyed, over-it, can't-be-bothered, novelty-has-worn-off thoughts. I'm aware that they're negative thoughts, and I know that I shouldn't pay too much heed to them or let them rule me. But right now I don't care. I just feel tired and grumpy.

On the screen, the Viking leader is heading a gruesome raid on England, his fearless missus by his side. I wish I was a warrior queen kicking arse back in the day with my braided hair flying. But I'm not. I'm a lumpy, bumpy, middle-aged housewife with a head full of First World problems. I feel fat (ice cream), moody (hormones), tired (everything) and sorry for myself (basic self-absorption). I am far from a Zen housewife.

Why? Because life keeps happening. People keep saying and doing tricky, confusing, hurtful things. My kids keep being demanding and challenging. I still have moods and emotions that are painful and uncomfortable. Things don't go according to plan. Pressures arise. I still have to live sober in a booze-soaked world. People I love get sick. I get sick. Deadlines loom. Tense work meetings occur.

It's all very well having an understanding of how my mind works and knowing some mindfulness techniques to help me control it, but putting it all into practice day in, day out, as life swirls around me, is another matter.

I'm finding it impossible to spend all my days blissing out at nature or thinking about the air in my lungs. I need to clean toilets, fold washing, cook meals and drive places. I need to be on the internet, writing blogs, running my websites and updating my social media accounts. I need to interact with other people all the time and some of them are dickheads. I need to try to be a good mother, wife, sister, daughter, friend. How can I marry all of this busy and stressful life stuff with a solid mindfulness practice? It's just too hard!

I tear my eyes away from the swarthy humans on the screen, flip the book open and read: 'Negative spirals are incredibly powerful. You can begin to dissipate them just by becoming aware of them. The simple act of turning towards and observing them helps to dissolve such patterns.'

Goddammit.

These guys just seem to know how to hook me in.

As much as I want to give up on this stuff and wallow in my self-indulgent misery, I've still got this deep yearning for something to change. And I know that if I change nothing then nothing will change. I've had a few teeny-tiny glimpses of the calm feelings mindfulness can generate—subtle feelings, but discernible nonetheless—and my social media feeds are still bombarding me with messages about how effective it is. I know deep down that I've got to keep going with it. What is becoming abundantly clear is that this isn't going to be the quick fix I was hoping for. Grasping the concepts isn't enough—I'm pretty sure I have to actually put them into regular practice too.

With half an eye on the Vikings' magnificent bodies (bet they don't have sugar binges) I reach for the iPad and type: *Do you have to practise mindfulness regularly for it to work?* Google leads me back to that guy Joseph Goldstein, who first introduced me to the concept of thoughts being like little energy bubbles in the mind. He confirms that, just as you need to brush your teeth regularly to keep them clean, you have to practise mindfulness regularly to keep your mind clean.

> It's not as if you get the teachings and then it's a linear path upwards to greater and greater enlightenment. There are a lot of ups and downs on the path. There are times when we forget. A common pitfall is for people even to get discouraged, in the face of that or begin to doubt or to have self-judgment. These ups and downs are part of the path. Everybody goes through them.

Well thanks, Mr Goldstein. You've just made me feel much better about being over it and discouraged right now.

On the telly, a Viking is strung up while the skin on his back is sliced open and peeled off. Bloody hell, those were bloody times. Blood is everywhere! It's getting a bit much, to be honest. I focus back on the iPad and read more from Joseph, who is not peeling skin but rather reassuring me by saying that stopping, starting, coming and going from mindfulness is normal. Well, thank goodness for that. He then says something that really resonates with me: the times when we do stop practising, or get stuck, or start to ruminate on things, or go through a struggle where we act 'reactively rather than responsively' are the times that can teach us the most.

I like the feeling that I'm learning something about myself

when I lurch messily through a tricky time. Although, exactly what I've just learned from my trying day, I'm unsure. And what does acting reactively rather than responsively even mean? I need to find out.

Half an hour, a lot of Viking blood and many Google searches later, I have the answer. Reactive is bad; responsive is good. Acting reactively is bad because it means you're making a quick judgement or action based on immediate, surface feelings, without pausing to give the wise, calm part of yourself a chance to be involved. Acting responsively, on the other hand, is much better because it means you are pausing to take stock (and drawing on mindfulness techniques will help do this), giving yourself time to respond in a calmer and more considered way. Reactive is hard; responsive is soft.

I've since heard of many different mindfulness techniques— each with a nifty acronym—that are designed to help you to respond, rather than react.

First there's the RAIN technique:

Recognise what's here
Allow what's here to be here
Investigate and inquire
Non-identification and natural awareness.

Then there's the STOP technique:

Stop

Take a few breaths

Observe

Proceed.

The SAFE technique:

Soften

Allow

Feel

Expand.

And finally the SOBER breathing space:

Stop

Observe

Breathe

Expand

Respond; don't react.

I can immediately see what all of these techniques are trying to get me to do: just slow the hell down and pause when something is happening, before acting or making any decisions. Sounds simple, but like a lot of this stuff it is easier said than done.

Well, bugger me if I don't feel like the mother of the year!

The very next morning, over breakfast, I have the perfect opportunity to practise responding and not reacting. It's a Monday, everyone is tired from the busy weekend we've had, and the kids are bickering while I'm filling their lunchboxes. A familiar battle breaks out between me and my middle son: he's refusing, again, to let me put sandwiches in his lunchbox. He is pacing around me, winding himself up. 'But I don't *like* them!' His energy is high.

I start doing what I always do, which is bring my own tense energy up to meet his. 'I'm *sorry* but you *need* sandwiches, otherwise once again you'll be *starving* and *grumpy* when I pick you up at three o'clock.'

This is our pattern: he rises up in protest, I rise up to meet him, and we end up going hammer and tongs at each other. Not fun.

'No I *won't!*' he is yelling now.

I'm about to yell back when I remember what I've been reading. Amazingly, I manage to catch myself.

Oh shit, I think. *I'm supposed to be pausing here. What do I do again?* I scrabble to remember one of the techniques. I can't remember much other than just stopping and pausing and breathing . . . so I force myself to do that. I stop buttering the bread, close my eyes and take a few deep breaths. My youngest son, who is sitting beside me calmly eating his Weet-Bix (he's witnessed this fight before), notices what I'm doing and says, 'Are you pretending to be dead, Mum?'

Still with my eyes closed, I giggle a bit, shake my head to let him know that no, I'm not pretending to be dead, and force myself to stay with the pause, taking another couple of deep breaths. I'm not thinking about anything specifically; I am just pausing. I'm familiar enough with focusing on my breath by now that I am able to clear my mind somewhat and just feel my chest rise and fall.

When I finally open my eyes again, my youngest son is staring at me in bemusement and grumpy middle boy is sitting on the floor pulling on his socks. I feel a bit different, there's no denying it. My shoulders have dropped a bit, I'm sure. And I don't really care about the sandwiches anymore. I just can't be bothered with the fight. But, more than that, the detail of our argument suddenly seems very unimportant and I find myself looking at the situation from a wider perspective.

Suddenly all I see is a very emotional little boy sitting on the floor, and I feel compassionate rather than angry with him. He's still so young. I feel like a super-calm mum and I say to him gently, 'Listen, you don't have to have sandwiches if you really hate them, but you need something substantial in your lunchbox that is going to fill you up properly. You can't have just biscuits and crackers. What else could you have?'

'I DON'T KNOW!' He's still locked in fight mode.

Little does he know, in the space of the last minute, I have magically morphed into a Zen mother. I keep my voice low (almost comedy low, like I'm acting) and say, 'Well, come and look for something. I'll help you.'

He must be able to detect the kindness in my voice because he responds a little more softly himself. 'OK,' he says (still with a bit of attitude—can't give up that easily) and comes over to the fridge. We run through a few options before he settles on some leftover pasta from last night's dinner, and with that the lunchbox drama is over.

Well, bugger me if I don't feel like the mother of the year! That was *super* satisfying, I have to admit. Who knew that just keeping my own energy low and my voice uber calm would work so brilliantly to mellow out my son and defuse our argument. I've been so locked into a pattern of behaviour I'd forgotten I had the power to change it.

It's a very profound sensation— surreal, magical even

As the days go on I keep listening to Mark's audios and practising mindfulness techniques, and as a result my mood stays fairly even. I generally feel that subtle-but-noticeable bit calmer and more on top of things. Content.

And also, now that I'm forcing myself to become more aware of what's happening in the precise moment I'm in, it's becoming amazingly clear to me that 99.9 per cent of the moments in my day are actually lovely and calm. Practically all of the time there is nothing fraught happening, I'm just walking down the steps with everything quiet around me, or putting the washing on with everything quiet and calm around me, or writing a blog with everything quiet and calm around me, or even interacting with my kids about ordinary, everyday stuff with nothing dramatic going on. Honestly, once I start really looking at it, most of my life is uneventful and nice. I never realised! It's really beginning to be rammed home to me how much drama I've been creating purely out of my own thinking. And to be able to let that drama go and just pop myself fully down into the moment I'm in—well, it's astonishingly calm and lovely. Exactly what I have been wanting my life to be like. I'm really on to something here.

I'm finally about to experience a little moment of awe.

It happens in my car. I'm parked up outside school. In fifteen minutes, the bell will go and I'll be surrounded by my boys and noise, but right now I'm listening to Mark's calm voice coming out of my phone. I've got my eyes shut and am feeling relaxed as I hear him tell me, 'The deep stillness we seek does not arise because the world is still or the mind is quiet. Stillness is nourished when we allow things to be just as they are for now. In this moment. Moment by moment, and breath by breath.'

I'm listening to Mark and not thinking about much except the sensations of my body and I must be totally in the zone because suddenly I experience what can only be described as quite a dramatic sensation where I enter the present moment and drop fully into my body. I have this almost shock-and-awe awareness of my 43-year-old body sitting in a car.

Clunk.

I feel a stillness and nothing else but being totally in my body, totally in this moment.

It's a very profound sensation—surreal, magical even.

Like, *wow*.

It's hard to put this experience into words, so I don't try to explain it to anyone around me; even when ten minutes later a mum by the school gates winks at me and says, 'Saw you sitting in your car just now, Lotta. Were you having a little private moment there?'

'Yes, I was!' I admit, but don't go into detail. Little does she know how private and significant my little moment was.

I carry this vivid clunking feeling with me in the days and weeks ahead (and I can still remember it clearly even now as I write this). I know in my heart it was significant, and I know it only came about because I refused to give up on trying to change my reality.

All of the work I've been doing on mindfulness is finally starting to have an impact as I move through my days. Slowly, slowly, as the concepts of mindfulness are being cemented in place, I'm noticing some really positive effects. The butterflies in my tummy have gone. I'm not going off on huge mental tangents, thinking of complex narratives about everything that is going on in my life. I just feel content and good—more at peace with everything overall. And slowly the sceptic inside me, who dismisses all this stuff as kooky and wishy-washy, is disappearing.

I'm realising now that someone who is into meditation or mindfulness is not, as I've always thought, a self-indulgent navel-gazer. They're the exact opposite. They're not sitting there thinking about themselves; they're sitting there distancing themselves from themselves! They're turning off autopilot mode, which is a mindless allegiance to a steady stream of thoughts, letting go of those thoughts and just *being*. It's phenomenal. I find a quote from Joseph Goldstein (fast becoming my number-one mindfulness guru) which sums up the scale of what I am feeling.

We're talking about a vast transformation of consciousness. We can have just a tremendous ... almost a sense of awe in the undertaking of the path. To be honest this is a huge thing, this is not a hobby, it's something that is our lives. It's the exploration of the nature of consciousness and what creates suffering and what are the avenues.

Yes, Joseph, I do have a sense of awe. And I do feel like my consciousness is being transformed. Tell me more!

I love the sense of bringing courage to the path, because it's that strength of heart that's willing to go through, and be with, the ups and downs and the difficulties.

Ah yes, the difficulties. The way life happens and my brain reverts to old, tight ways of thinking and processing things. I've already had an experience of this. I move forward with my mindfulness training, start to open up, calm down and feel great, then some tricky things occur and I get stuck again. But at least I'm still moving forward, right? My commitment to following Mark and Danny's eight-week plan is probably the main thing that is keeping me going, and stopping me from just reverting back to old ways, right now.

But, as I'm about to discover, even with a solid plan to follow, it's not so easy to keep going deeper and be all uber grounded and calm when you have to travel away from home to visit family and friends, and when you're constantly needing to interact, negotiate and make plans with other people.

Chapter 12

Oh, the freedom in letting my thoughts go

I'm about to be thrust out of my lovely, self-contained neighbourhood life and into social madness. We're heading away on holiday to my uncle's remote property to join loads of relatives for a fiesta of mixing, mingling, eating, drinking and family dynamics. I find family holidays are always a combination of wonderful and edgy. But this is the first time we've all got together since my step-father died, so I'm mostly just looking forward to seeing everyone again.

I'm also determined to try to spend the week as the most Zen version of myself I can possibly be. I'll try really hard to just go with the flow and not mentally grasp on to things. *Don't get caught up in your head, Lotta!* I tell myself. *Don't create unhelpful mental narratives about what other people are doing or saying, Lotta! Don't think too much, Lotta! Stay focused on what is happening right here in any given moment, Lotta! Stop talking to yourself, Lotta!*

As I get the suitcases out and start packing for the kids and myself, I decide I'm not going to discuss all this mindfulness stuff with family while I'm away. Corin knows what I'm up to by now, but no one else in my family does. I doubt anyone will want to have in-depth conversations with me about the nature of thought anyway, and even if they did I'm not sure I'd be up to having them. I've noticed that when I talk to Corin about what I'm discovering they are very difficult concepts to articulate. I've had a go at trying to put into words all that I am learning and the internal shift that is going on for me but I struggle to find the words to describe it, and judging by the look on his face at times, I don't think I'm getting it across very well. I'm far from being an expert on the subject.

No, I think as I scrounge around the house, trying to find the kids' wetsuits. *On this holiday, I'm just going to keep what I'm doing quietly to myself.* It all feels a bit new and precious to let out yet. So I'll keep it secret.

I'm a bit unsure about how I'm going to do this when I need to listen to Mark's audios every day. I can't have anyone catching me at it! I'll need to find a time to do it when I won't be spotted, and a good private location—hard when all five of us will be sharing a room all holiday.

I carefully select what clothes to pack, bundle up my iPad and phone chargers (can't be without technology!), put together a container full of tea bags (one of my regular self-care practices—I always take my favourite tea away with me), and pop in a couple of books in case I get some downtime to read (not likely with the kids to entertain, but I live in hope). One of the books I pop into my suitcase is by the comedian Ruby Wax. I picked it up at the library just the other day, because someone told me she'd moved away from the comedy realm and into the world of mental health and mindfulness. It's called *Sane New World: Taming the mind* and sounds right up my alley.

Bags packed, supplies ready, time to leave the nest.

My uncle's property is so remote it takes us two boat rides to get there. As we make our final approach—bobbing across the rough seas—I catch sight of the property and suddenly remember that he has the *perfect* spot for me to squirrel away and do my mindful thing: a treehouse! OMG, yes! Nestled in the bush up the back of his place is a super-cool, big, old treehouse. A rickety wooden staircase leads up to it, and there's a balcony at the top with a room off it filled with comfy old sofas. It's the perfect place.

So now the question is: when am I going to use it? There are nearly 30 people buzzing around this property while we are here and I don't want any of them interrupting my Zen. There's only one thing for it: I'm going to have to do what I've always fantasised about (in a very abstract don't-actually-want-to-do-it-in-reality way) and set my alarm for sparrow's fart.

And I actually do it! I set my alarm and get up at six every morning, while everyone else is asleep, and by torchlight I creep up to the treehouse in my nightwear and slippers. Once up there, I perch myself on the edge of the sofa—back straight but not stiff, signifying my intention to pay attention (see what I've learned!)—and I listen to Mark guide me in a meditation. It's a totally awesome experience to be sitting in a creaking and swaying treehouse as the sun comes up, listening to the calm, wise-sounding voice of Mark.

At this stage of the plan (Week Five), he's working to cement in my mind the idea that thoughts are not facts; they're just little 'mental events', little puffs of energy. With the sound of early-morning birdsong softly audible outside, I sit and listen as he reassures me.

> From time to time you might find that your mind gets caught up in your thinking, no longer observing your thoughts and feelings, but lost inside them. When this happens congratulate yourself for waking up, taking a moment to acknowledge what your mind got caught in, then beginning again, renewing your

intention to observe these mental events as they arise, stay a while, then dissolve.

Oh, the freedom in letting my thoughts go. This really is what I've been wanting.

Starting each day like this is utterly lovely, and every time I make my way back down from the treehouse and into the busy and stimulating group environment I feel happy and calm. And it's probably no coincidence that I'm finding this holiday much easier than past ones—I'm not doing my usual fretting about family stuff.

I'm not bothered by being the sober elephant in the room either, unlike in past years when I've found everyone else's daily drinking to be quite a challenge. I'm not worrying about how little anyone knows about what I'm going through in my life. I'm not stressing about things I have no control over, like tensions between other family members. I'm just feeling good. And, because my own mind is calm, I'm much more able to tune in with what is going on for everyone else. I'm sure I'm listening better and holding space for others. Everything is just a bit easier to manage. It's grand.

Grand, that is, until we discover that my four-year-old nephew brought a nasty tummy bug with him on holiday and it has been spreading itself around the group. Slowly, we all get hit with the most violent vomiting bug known to humankind. It is a shocker! One by one, we drop like flies and disappear into our rooms to recover. Here I was thinking this holiday would go down in memory as being my Awesome Treehouse Meditation Holiday, but now it looks like it will forever be remembered as the Tummy Bug From Hell Holiday.

It's similar to having a Ferrari except no one gave you the keys

There is one good thing to be said for tummy bugs and bed rest, though (aside from the tiny bit of weight loss!): it allows for long periods of uninterrupted reading. I get stuck into Ruby Wax's book as I quarantine myself off to recuperate. Luckily, Corin and I have no overlap in our illnesses so we can take turns looking after the kids while the other one is laid up. It's actually very nice. Not the vomiting—that's not very nice at all—but the lying around in silence recuperating is.

And luckily Ruby is a great bed companion. (I mean that in the least creepy way possible.) I'm finding her book a rollicking good read—funny and informative and right in my wheelhouse. She's brutally honest about her struggles with depression and her career path, which has seen her go from comedy writing and celebrity interviewing to psychotherapy, neuroscience and mindfulness. I'm jealous as all hell to discover that she studied under my friend Mark (aka Professor Mark Williams) at Oxford

University! Oh boy, I wish I could do that! I fantasise from my sickbed about moving to the UK to do a second Masters in Mindfulness-based Cognitive Therapy, just like Ruby has. Mark and I could discuss raisins, he'd praise me for my astounding insights...

Ruby leads me into the world of the human brain and unpicks how it works. She calls it a 'pliable, three-pound piece of play dough' and has nifty cartoon drawings showing me all the different parts and what they do. In between naps, I read about lobes and cortexes and chemicals (luckily she's pretty adept at making the science-y stuff accessible, even to someone like me who failed science at school). And she intersperses all the 'heavy' stuff with amusing (and sometimes awful) anecdotes from her own crazy life.

She confirms something I've been aware of since I got sober and started investigating addiction and recovery: that we have the power to change our minds and how we think. This is called neuroplasticity, a word I've always rather liked because it sounds both brainy and childlike at the same time. I know firsthand how neuroplasticity works, because I have experienced a monumental turnaround in my own thinking: I completely reshaped and rewired my grey matter when it came to my alcohol addiction. Where I used to experience intense and overwhelming urges to drink whenever any sort of emotional high or low (or 5pm on a Tuesday) came along, nowadays I *never* do. Like NEVER. Incredible! I used to be a complete slave to alcohol, but now I am entirely free of the stuff. Neuroplasticity in action.

Now Ruby is telling me that practising mindfulness regularly can also have a major positive impact on how your brain is shaped and how it functions—and she's got the data to prove it. I flick to the back of her book where she has listed the results of numerous studies that prove what profound changes practising mindfulness can bring to bear. These aren't silly questionnaires carried out by school kids over the internet; they are reputable studies by researchers from institutions such as UCLA, Stanford, Harvard, the University of Pennsylvania and the Yale School of Medicine. These pointy heads have pulled together hard evidence to show how practising mindfulness can help people do such things as reduce their pain sensitivity, change their baseline levels of happiness and optimism, reduce their depression, reduce the reactivity in the amygdala (the area of the brain usually overactive in highly anxious people), manage their addictive behaviours, reduce their stress-related heart and stomach pain, reduce their distracted thoughts, increase their ability to let go of the negative rumination process, and develop a positive state of mind. This has all been proven by researchers at universities, for goodness' sake!

Wow. The more I learn, the more I realise that mindfulness is a total game-changer for us humans. Given its overwhelming positive outcomes (some of which I have started experiencing for myself) I'm beginning to wonder why it isn't way more mainstream. It should be a compulsory part of school curricula everywhere, prescribed by doctors, ordered by the courts. Mindfulness centres should be as prevalent as bars—imagine the reduction in alcohol-related harm if everyone went to a lovely Zen environment after work to naturally calm themselves, rather than to a bar to imbibe toxic liquids that numb true emotions and create artificial feelings of wellbeing.

Imagine if mindfulness centres were as commonplace as gyms, and everyone worked as hard on their ability to ground themselves in the moment as they did on their ability to lift weights. Some might think B-O-R-I-N-G! But I don't think life would be boring if you felt generally calm and at peace most of the time. And I think that all of these habits can be embedded into a life. Why not go to the gym *and* the mindfulness centre *and* the bar for a quiet drink or two (soda with a twist of lime for me, thanks!).

Lying in my sickbed, I decide that practising mindfulness regularly is a no-brainer (no pun intended). Why wouldn't I want to keep doing something that, as I have already discovered, has a tangible impact on my day-to-day experience of life? The only reason not to would be if it resulted in me losing my personality and becoming a boring-ass nun. Ruby reassures me it won't, though: 'This does not mean you sit there like a lump of tofu with a bindi on your head, listening to the sitar; it means when your mind does what all of our minds do, which is change—change constantly and never stop chattering—you don't fight it but rather understand and accept it for what it is.'

Why haven't I been doing this already?

Why haven't I spent my life being aware that my thoughts are nothing more than energy bubbles that don't necessarily need to be paid attention to?

Why have I let my thoughts put me on edge and create butterflies in my belly?

Why have I let my thoughts wind me up about inter-personal situations that aren't really that bad?

Why have I let my thoughts ruin perfectly calm days by making me obsessively ruminate over things in the past or the future?

Why have I gone through so many days not paying full attention to what is going on right before my very eyes?

Why am I only now, at the age of 43, starting to realise that I have the power to radically alter how I experience the world and my place in it simply by slowing down and making space to ground myself in my awareness and to distance myself from my steady stream of thoughts?

I know the answer: it's because I was never given the tools to do this until now. I remember Dan Harris writing about this in his book: 'Our minds have this other capability—a bonus level, to put it in gamerspeak—that no one ever tells us about in school. (Not here in the West, at least.) We can do more than just think; we also have the power simply to be aware of things—without judgment, without the ego.'

And now Ruby is backing him up, explaining how complex and incredible our brains are, but how little we know about using them. She says it's similar to having a Ferrari except no one gave you the keys.

Is she having a deep and meaningful moment with the cobwebs on the ceiling?

I start thinking of the big blob of grey play dough not just in my own head but in the heads of everyone around me. When I finally emerge from my sickbed and get back to mingling with the family (each of whom are also slowly emerging from their sickbeds), I find myself strangely hyper-aware of the minds of everyone on holiday with me. I'm rather fascinated that we all own these incredibly clever 'Ferrari' brains (thanks, Ruby) with a 'bonus level' (thanks, Dan) where we can slip behind the endless mind-chatter and simply observe life with no running commentary added. Yet none of us have ever been taught about this—well, not in my society, anyway. We're all just amateur drivers or novice gamers (depending on which metaphor you favour), gritting our teeth through life, being slaves to our inner dialogues. By crikey, it's no wonder everyone drinks alcohol all the time and lives in an edgy, stressed-out way!

Actually that's a bit presumptuous. Maybe it's just me who has spent most of my adult life unaware that I had the ability to stop my inner dialogue and calm myself by focusing on what's actually happening in the moment. Maybe other people— including some of my relatives around me now—do hold the key to stopping their endless thinking cycles and dropping into mindful awareness of the present moment. Maybe it's just me who is only now waking up to the incredible ability I have to stop the ceaseless adherence to my inner dialogue.

As I stand in the kitchen, watching my uncle fry eggs, I start wondering, *Is he holding that frying-pan in full consciousness right now, marvelling at the yellowness of the yolks and the sizzling of the oil? Or is he busy up in his head, worrying about the troublesome staff member he needs to fire next week?*

'Eggs are ready!' he bellows to the gathering throng.

My cousin's partner enters the room ('Feeling OK?' 'Much better, thanks!') and starts mashing a banana for her baby daughter. *Is she marvelling at the sensation of the fork pressing through the ripe flesh, and the bright images on her daughter's plate? Or is she stressing over something a friend said last week?*

I catch my sister staring off into the distance. *Is she having a deep and meaningful moment with the cobwebs on the ceiling?*

Or is she worrying about her son's fussy food habits?

Who knows what everyone is thinking at any one time?

It's seems incredible to me, as I look around, that every one of my family members is viewing the world from a perspective where they are the star of the movie. They're the hero of their own story, walking around with their own thoughts giving them a running commentary on everything that is happening. And, at any particular point in time, their movie could be a romance, a horror, a documentary, or even a depressing tear-jerker.

Unless someone lets me in on what they're truly thinking (and that rarely happens), I can't possibly know what their version of reality is. Nor do I need to know—their truth is theirs alone, unless they decide to share it. But still, I have to be honest, it is calming for me to sit here now and be aware that everyone else is a slave to their own thoughts too. It helps me to think of others, not just of myself. It breaks me out of my own running commentary, or at least helps me to put it into perspective. It's not facts; it's just my version of events based on my current state of mind. And everyone is doing the same thing up in their own heads.

Actually, truth be told, right now they're probably all just thinking about the nasty bug that has had us all laid up. As I break myself out of my own internal dialogue about what everyone else is thinking about (not very mindful, that!), I tune into the conversation going on around me, and discover it's mostly a comparison of how many times everyone has vomited in the past 24 hours. There is nothing like a tummy bug to help family members bond.

Chapter 13

If I just stop telling myself over and over that I'm busy and tired, will I really feel less busy and less tired?

As we head home after our mini break I'm feeling good and calm, which isn't always the case after big family holidays. This time, I didn't find myself getting all angsty about tense undercurrents that are out of my control, and my mood stayed even. I'm convinced this is a direct result of the mindfulness research and reading and practising I'm doing. (Being sober always helps, too—no hangovers or regret to bring me down like in the bad old days.) And I'm really proud of myself that, despite the tummy bug, I kept regularly listening to Mark's audios. Every day, mostly in the treehouse and sometimes in my sickbed, his dulcet tones were there to remind me that I can slip into a calm mindset by recognising my thoughts, by letting them go without judgement, and by focusing on my breath and my body. Words don't do justice to my experience of doing this; it really is remarkably calming.

I'm a bit nervous, though. In the weeks ahead, I think I'm going to struggle to maintain my lovely, mindful momentum. I've just finished Mark and Danny's eight-week plan, and right at the same time Corin is heading away overseas on a big work trip—to a scary war zone, no less. Corin's absence is not only going to increase my workload considerably, but I also tend to get edgy when he's out of the house and I don't sleep as well as I normally do (sober me usually gets a good eight hours of un-broken sleep every night—not something I ever achieved with a belly full of wine!). Parenting and housework feel even more relentless than normal when I can't palm some of it off on to him occasionally.

Usually all of this extra busyness is accompanied by a noisy internal dialogue in which I moan to myself about how busy I am and how hard it is running things alone while he's gone. This time, though, I'm hoping that I can lessen my load by reaching for the new tool in my toolbox: mindfulness. Can it be that simple? If I just stop telling myself over and over that I'm busy and tired, will I really feel less busy and less tired?

I bloody hope so!

I cry when Corin leaves, but as soon as his taxi has driven away I pull myself together and tell myself to get on with it—and there's a lot to be getting on with.

Although the eight-week course is over, Mark's audios are still on my phone, so I occasionally drive to school fifteen minutes early and listen to him in the car while I wait for the boys. But, in all honesty, I'm not doing it that often. Truth is, if I'm not cleaning or cooking or driving the kids around, I'm online, busy interacting, updating, uploading, posting and publishing. I'm aware that the internet isn't a very mindful place to hang out, and that my overuse of technology probably isn't improving my general state of mind, but I don't actually care. I *love* my online world. It's important to me. Everything I do online is either work, fun or (unnecessary but entertaining) distractions.

I'm struggling to see how mindfulness and technology can work together anyway. To be mindful online, should I simply be surfing the web more slowly? Should I be taking my time to fully appreciate humorous memes and video clips? That doesn't seem right.

The internet is a hard one for me, actually, because not only is it a great distraction when I'm feeling edgy but it has also been a crucial part of my sobriety. I often joke that the internet saved my liver—but, in truth, this ain't no joke. If I hadn't started blogging, I might never have discovered what a powerful thing it is to get my thoughts and feelings out of my head and written out. When I was deep in my addiction, I kept so many of my twisted ideas and secret behaviours hidden inside myself. Typing out my shitty truths and dysfunctional, addictive habits made it much easier to deal with—and to ultimately free myself from—them.

Of course, there was also the added bonus of being drawn into the wonderful online recovery community—a community I remain a firm member of to this day. Ninety-nine percent of my sober friends and support networks are online, and every single day since I put down the bottle I have reached out through my keyboard to connect with other addicts in recovery, by sharing tips and truths, and finding strength and inspiration.

So yeah, the internet is a ginormous and wonderful part of my life, but it does have its downsides.

I can get emotionally affected if someone posts something that I find confronting or hurtful—for example, if an actor I admire is constantly posting pictures of booze, or if a neighbourhood mum posts photos from a barbecue I wasn't invited to. Also, my body can complain about my internet usage through a sore neck, sore eyes and sore wrists. And it's certainly not very mindful to be busy scrolling through Instagram instead of paying attention to a real-life person right in front of me—especially a small, grumpy person who is desperately trying to get my attention.

I feel a bit geeky doing this, like I'm some sort of touchy-feely parent from the 1970s

The small person in question in this instance is my middle son, and he's raving about something that is wrong with his life. I drag my focus away from someone's photo of their birthday flowers and launch into my usual response: I tell him that I try my best to keep everything fair, and that, despite what he may think about his brothers getting a better deal than him, it usually all comes out evenly in the end.

'But he had *more* than me!' he wails.

'No he didn't.' I sigh. 'And anyway you'll get more later.'

Honestly, we've been around this goat track before. He always manages to find some way in which he feels he's being unfairly disadvantaged, some thing that he can use to prove he's missing out yet again. I'm told this is very common 'middle-child syndrome' behaviour.

As he's pacing around in front of me, I feel myself get all reactive.

'Stop looking at what's wrong all the time,' I snap. (He's not listening.)

'Flip your thinking.' (He's still not listening.)

'Try looking at all the good things right now instead of what you think is bad.' (*Still* not listening, and now lying on the floor with his face in a beanbag.)

Then suddenly I remember: I need to pause and breathe! *Be a mindful mummy, Lotta!* So I do just that. I close my eyes and I take two deep breaths. Then I open my eyes again and it dawns on me—what this guy needs is to practise some goddam gratitude. He needs help training his brain not to look for the negatives all the time, and to focus on the positives instead. Maybe I can help him with that? But how?

I leave the room to go and put the jug on. A cup of tea will help me think (a cup of tea helps me with everything). As I wait for the water to boil, I come up with a plan. Bedtime would be the best ... We could use the time when I'm tucking him in every night to list some good things about the day. I grab a mug out of the cupboard. Yes! That's it! A bedtime gratitude practice. I'm jazzed by the idea, because I know it will help me too. My Happiness Bowl may be dearly departed, but I'm aware that I should still be regularly practising gratitude myself. I grab a teabag (my favourite: green tea with mandarin), pop it in a mug and pour hot water over it. I walk back into the TV room, where my son is still lying face down in the beanbag—no doubt running over and over in his mind all that is terrible in the world.

'I'm going to start a gratitude practice with you,' I announce decisively. 'To help you shift your focus on to all the good things in your life.'

'Mumble, mumble' is all I hear. I'm sure he has no idea what I'm on about.

Later that night, I follow through with my idea. He's snuggled up under the bed covers, all calm now and smelling sweet from a bath. I sit on the edge of his bed and say to him, 'Right, so... what are three things that you're grateful for today?' I feel a bit geeky doing this, like I'm some sort of touchy-feely parent from the 1970s.

He must think me odd too, as he looks at me strangely. 'What?' he asks.

'Three things—any three things—that were good about your day today,' I explain. 'Can you tell me them?'

I can see he's interested in this game. He appears to take a while to think about it—or maybe he's just thinking what a nutter I am. Then, lo and behold, it turns out he's not going to resist me, but is in fact keen to play along. *Very* keen!

'Um... I got to play *Plants Vs. Zombies: Garden Warfare* after dinner,' he starts with.

'Good one!' I say.

'Um... I got to FaceTime call Dad.'

'Yep... and?'

'And... it's nearly my birthday.'

'Awesome!'

We smile at each other.

Then he says, 'Your turn.'

Oh crikey. 'Ah...OK...I'm grateful that Dad FaceTimed us,' I say. It was really nice to see Corin safe, and alive, after his trip reporting from the scary war zone. 'And I'm grateful that he'll be home soon.'

'Yep,' my son says. We're clearly in agreement.

'I had a good meeting about my work today, and ...' I look out the door to the kids' rumpus room and the secondhand pool table we've recently added to it. 'I'm grateful we've got a really cool house.'

He smiles. 'Yeah!'

We're both feeling good.

'That was fun!' I say, giving him a kiss on the cheek. 'We'll do this every night from now on.'

'OK,' he says sleepily, as I exit the room.

The next night we do the same thing—same time, same place. I'm sitting on the edge of my son's bed, and he's all snuggled up and cosy.

'OK, what are your three things that you're grateful for today?' I ask.

He immediately answers, 'I had fun at school today.'

'Oh, that's good!' I say.

'I got to talk to Grandma on the phone.'

'Nice one,' I say.

'And it's nearly my birthday.'

'Yes it is!' I'm impressed by how easily he has taken to this.

'Your turn,' he says.

'OK...um...I did some good writing today. I'm grateful for the jug that is about to boil water for my cup of tea...and I am grateful for my family.'

I walk out of his room feeling very lovely.

The next night when I tuck him in, I give him a kiss and move to leave the room—I've completely forgotten our little gratitude practice. I'm about to start climbing the stairs when I hear him call out to me, 'Three things!'

Shit, I forgot. 'Sorry!' I make my way back to sit on the edge of his bed, and we each find three good things about each of our days.

Just like that, we kick off a long-standing and remarkable habit. As I write this book, this 'Three Things' gratitude practice has become a firm fixture in our house, and a great tool in my toolbox. It has spread to my number-three son as well. (I've tried to get number one into it, but he won't play ball—I think you've got to get it going with kids while they're still young and malleable.) Every night, when I tuck the two younger boys into bed, we do our Three Things. Many items are repeated. 'I had a good day at school' is often mentioned, as is 'I've got the best family/house/friends in the world'. I often say, 'I'm grateful that I get to be your mum,' and 'I did some good writing today,' and lately (since I've been writing this book, actually, which has helped remind me that it's good to keep this one foremost in my mind), 'I'm grateful that I'm sober.'

There's absolutely no doubt in my mind that this bedtime routine has benefitted all of us who play along. It's the cumulative effect that makes it so powerful, rather than the individual evenings. Finding things to feel positive about night after night after night gives you an overall sense that life is pretty bloody good, even though it hurts and is tough a lot of the time. Even on my shittiest days, I can usually come up with something (even if it's simply 'I'm grateful for the fridge that keeps our food cold'). That's the amazing thing: there is *always* something to be grateful for. Previously, in times of stress and grumpiness, I would never have naturally brought them to mind on a daily basis.

I have to admit now that the person who tweeted 'Listing what I am grateful for is a practice that contributes to a sense of joy and peace' was bang on the money. Listing what I'm grateful for is indeed a practice that contributes to me feeling joy and peace. It's such a simple thing to do, and our nightly Three Things habit has become a contributing factor to my ability to cope with life in the raw—and, given that tricky stuff is always happening, I'll take every little bit of help I can get.

MY TOOLBOX

Recovery community

Sober treats

Mindfulness

Gratitude practice (Three Things)

Carrots really are a remarkable shade of orange, flies are busy little creatures and clouds can be satisfyingly dramatic

My fledgling mindfulness practice, along with my new Three Things bedtime routine, is having a really positive impact on my days. Thanks to the influence these activities have on my thinking, I feel far better-equipped to deal with niggly stuff when it happens. As a result, I am feeling better able to stay on an even keel emotionally. I haven't felt any nagging sense of impending doom for a while, but I do still have a tendency to every now and then slip back into old mental habits where I get stuck going over and over something in my mind. The difference now is that I notice pretty quickly when I'm doing this. Before, I would just be thinking away—ruminating or worrying or planning—without being aware of what I was doing. Now, I still get caught in the same thinking loops, but it's like there's a new character inside my head, keeping watch, who pipes up to let me know when I'm getting stuck. 'You've been ruminating on that email for long enough,' she'll say, and then she'll point out something else I could be focusing my attention on. 'Why not look closely at those pretty leaves on the path as you walk up to the car?'

She's very interested in the minute detail of what is going on around me, this Internal Observer.

'Why don't you stop that imaginary conversation with that tricky person and marvel at those carrots you're chopping?'

'That concern about your sister could be shelved right now. Look! A fly crawling across the window!'

'Stop ruminating over how hard you're working. Check out those dramatic clouds rolling in from the east.'

The funny thing is that, when I force myself to focus on the physical things around me, I discover that carrots really are a remarkable shade of orange, flies are busy little creatures and clouds can be satisfyingly dramatic. And thoughts can be stopped. Who knew?

I like to picture my Internal Observer sitting on a chair in the corner of my mind, all cute in a retro dress and groovy glasses, and holding a notebook and pen. She even pipes up when I'm in bed at night. 'You checked Twitter eight minutes ago. Why don't you put the iPad down now and read your book?' (Sometimes I just ignore her.)

Aside from her nagging about my constant internet-surfing, I like this new observer in my mind. She's smart and helpful, and boy do I need her. Corin's still away, and despite feeling much calmer with my new techniques, I'm still bloody tired and rundown. Unfortunately, despite Ruby having informed me that studies prove mindfulness can improve people's immune systems, my practice clearly isn't kick-ass enough yet to shield me from bugs. Right before Corin gets home, I get sick—a nasty recurring infection in my leg that I can't ignore. I get myself to the doctor.

Sitting in the waiting room, I try not to do what I usually do here, which is practise over and over in my head what I'm going to say to the doctor when we finally get face-to-face (and in the process wind myself up about poor, sick me). Instead, I look around at all the other sickos in the waiting room and wonder what's going on with them. *What are their inner dialogues saying? Are they also repeating to themselves how tired and rundown they feel and how hard their lives are? Are they running over and over in their minds what they're about to say to the doctor?*

An elderly man looks up from his newspaper and catches me staring at him. He looks grumpy. *Shit! Hope he doesn't know I was trying to read his mind.*

I look down at my feet and try to breathe deeply and focus on the carpet, but it's hard to quieten my mind. After about a nanosecond, I stop trying to be mindful and just let the woe-is-me thoughts come flying at me unchecked. My mind is a veritable feast of self-indulgent thoughts right now. *Nobody realises how hard I work all the time. I'm racing around like a mad woman, doing so much. I deserve a break. My body is telling me I'm overworked. Poor me, getting sick. I am so hard done by. I do so much for everyone else . . .*

My Internal Observer is chewing her pen, unhappy that I'm letting my thoughts wind me up, but I don't care. I am bloody tired and sick and worn out and feeling sorry for myself, and I just want to wallow!

When the doctor finally appears to call out my name I've got myself so wound up about my illness that all she has to do once the door has shut behind us is ask me kindly 'What's up?' and I burst into tears. Oh gawd! Embarrassment! She hands me a tissue from the box conveniently placed on the edge of her desk, and I sniff my way through a jumbled explanation (this is *not* how I had practised it in my mind!).

'Sorry—*sniff*—it's just that I'm really tired—*sniff, sniff*—Corin is away right now and I've got a lot on. I'm just really busy—*sniff, sniff*—and my leg has got infected again. It's really sore and I'm worried that you'll have to cut it again.'

All she's probably hearing is 'leg' and 'infected', but she is sympathetic and asks me if I've been keeping well in general. 'Have you been feeling OK other than the infection?'

I've pulled myself together a bit now and manage to say, without crying, 'Yeah, mostly. Not sleeping great, but I never do when he's away. My food choices could probably be better, but I'm still not drinking any alcohol, of course.'

It always feels great to tell medical professionals that I don't drink—one of the highlights of sobriety!

She nods and makes some notes.

And then I say, 'Actually I've been practising some mindfulness stuff, and it's been really helpful, so I'm a bit bummed to have got rundown and sick.'

She looks up from her computer and really focuses her attention on me. 'Oh, that's good,' she says enthusiastically. 'It's a real life-changer.'

I feel proud, as though I've just got a gold star from the teacher. Yes! It *is* something to be proud of!

Ten minutes later, she's checked me out and is writing a prescription for antibiotics. I've relaxed completely by now and ask, 'Do you get a lot of teary housewives in here?'

She looks at me and nods. 'A lot.' She points to the tissue box sitting on the edge of her desk. 'I go through at least two of those a week.'

'Wowsers. That's a lot of teary patients!' I feel strangely calmed by the knowledge that there have been so many other stressed-out and snotty patients sitting on this chair before me, and that there will be many more after me as well. Similarly to when Ruby had me thinking about the thoughts of others while I was on holiday with my family, I'm finding that thinking of others is really quite comforting.

I leave the doctor resolving to think less about myself and my busy existence (which is totally normal and fine really; mine is a life full of First World problems). It's so easy for me to get bogged down by the little things, but it's helpful to remember that practically everyone else is also crazy busy and struggling in some way.

As I drive home I peer furtively into other cars to see the faces of the people driving them, imagining many of them being busy like I am, with their busy brains thinking all the time, running around after their kids, managing their careers and their households and their health and their finances and their social networks ...

Everyone is doing it hard in one way or another, not just me. Everyone is struggling along with a million things to do. Everyone is trying to get by as best they can. Reminding myself of this helps to lift me out of my own self-absorbed woes. *I must remember not to get so bogged down by my own story in future,* I tell myself.

By the time Corin returns home safe and sound (both he and his flak jacket all in one piece) I am on the mend physically and—I'm happy to say—I'm also doing well mentally. This is not usually the case when he gets back from an overseas trip:

normally I'm happy to see him but tense and strung out (and, if I'm honest, a little bitter that he's been travelling the world while I've been left slogging away at home). But this time, even with my sickness and the teary trip to the doctors, I've been able to keep myself feeling OK. This is undoubtedly due to the new tools in my toolbox.

I'm sure Corin is happy that he hasn't arrived home to a grumpy-wife-from-hell, but who would know? He's so exhausted from his own hard slog that he can barely think straight. It feels good to be the one to keep things running while he takes a day or two to recover. I know this sounds like nothing much, but I'm acutely aware that it is a new, very different mode of operating for me. I feel calmer and more positive than normal, and I feel in control of my world. This is exactly what I wanted when I first embarked on my mission to save myself!

And little do I know that, in the weeks ahead, an amazingly powerful (albeit very hairy) mental-health tool is about to arrive in my life.

Chapter 14

The most adorable
recovery tool around

I'm at home one morning, writing an impassioned blog post for
the Living Sober community about the addictive voice ('That
nasty, lying, conniving voice, your inner addict; the part of your
brain that wants you to keep imbibing alcohol to feed the addiction'), when the phone rings. It's a friend and she sounds excited.

'Hey, Lotta!' she greets me. 'You know how you said you guys
might be interested in getting a dog?'

'Um, yeah…' It's true: I did mention it in passing, but largely
because I'm getting bored with my friends having puppy
conversations that I can't join in on.

She continues breathlessly, 'Well, my breeder just called and they've got a little three-month-old black lab that urgently needs a home.'

'OK...' I reply slowly, already guessing where this is going.

'He went to a family, but apparently the mum put her foot down after just a few days and said she couldn't handle him—'

(This doesn't sound good.)

'So he's been sent back to the breeders and he needs a new family!'

I don't really know what to say, so I slowly repeat, 'OK...'

This is out of the blue, to say the least. However, the truth is that—my friends' endless puppy conversations aside—there has been some discussion recently between me and my boys about getting a dog. They're as keen as mustard, of course, and I've started feeling more positive about it, too. When I was young, my family had a golden retriever called Sam, who we all absolutely adored. (I can still remember being in London and getting a teary phone call from my mum and sister when he died. I drank a lot of whiskey that night to mourn him because, you know, that was my best way of coping with grief at the time.)

Also, I've been reading Arianna Huffington's book *Thrive* recently, and along with her tips for avoiding burnout and her praise of sleep (that's her big thing—she calls herself a sleep enthusiast), she has a big section on the wonders of owning a pet. She quotes numerous studies that prove pets not only open our hearts and enhance our lives, but have also been shown to lower blood pressure and stress levels, reduce the risk of heart disease, boost self-esteem, reduce feelings of loneliness, and increase fitness levels. She even points out that pets are naturally incredibly mindful! Animals, she says, are focused on the world right in front of them, in the present moment, and are more grounded in the world than so many of us humans, who are so busy rushing through that we never notice it properly.

Maybe this phone call from my friend was meant to be, coming at this exact point in my life when I'm trying to calm myself by connecting with the world around me? We could rescue this poor, rejected fella and bring him into our family...

Bugger it! Why not?

'I'd be keen, and I know the boys would too,' I tell my friend. 'But Corin might take some convincing.'

'Call him!'

'All right. Will do.'

Six hours later, we have a new, furry family member. Seriously—it happens that quickly. As it turns out, Corin doesn't need much convincing. He finishes work early, and we surprise the kids at the school gate with a 'We're going to look at a puppy!' (They practically burst out of their skins.) We then drive to the breeder's house, take one look at the cutest little black bundle of joy any of us have ever seen in our lives and instantly fall in love. He comes home with us immediately, snuggled in

Corin's arms in the front of the car. We spend the entire car ride home trying to pick out a name for him.

'Flash?'

'Midnight?'

'Stanley?'

'Stanley! Yes!'

It's unanimous.

We are so ill-prepared for Stanley. We have no bed for him, or chew toys, or even a fence to keep him in our backyard. But we have love, and that's all that matters. (And Corin takes Monday off work to build a fence.)

Since owning Stanley, I have discovered that Arianna was absolutely right when she described animals as the 'masters of giving back'—they give to us unconditionally and with the greatest pleasure. And, in the process, they teach us to do the same. It is impossible for us not to love Stanley, because he is so busy showering us with love himself. His interests are simple: food, exercise and buckets of love. He is like a never-ending love sponge. He's always there, right beside us, pushing his nose into our hands, looking up with his big eyes that plead, 'Love me, love me, love me!' at the same time as they promise, 'I love you, I love you, I love you!' It's impossible not to let his adoration and positive energy rub off.

And Stanley does more than just add many extra layers of love to our family; he has also done wonders for me on a personal level, both physically and mentally. Since I'm the only one at home during weekdays, I'm the one who has to walk him. Stanley gets me out of the house and into nature every day. It's new for me to be walking among greenery on a regular basis—whenever I have gone through phases of exercising regularly, it has always been at a gym, not outdoors. Stanley's pleading eyes and my desire to be a good dog owner are all it takes for me to tear myself away from the computer or stove or laundry basket and head off into the hills behind our house. We roam the paths together, Stanley scampering around me with unbridled joy, his tail wagging non-stop. There is no way I'd be up in the hills if it wasn't for Stanley—I'm way too lazy and comfortable at home to do this purely for myself.

As it happens, these walks are about more than just exercise. I've discovered that getting outside with this ball of canine energy is a brilliant time to practise mindfulness and to focus on being in the moment. Stanley is always leading the way with his inbuilt mindful attitude—running around, snuffling at the ground, chasing birds and barking at the wind. He's not wondering whether people like him, or what he's going to do tomorrow. He's fully immersed in his present-moment experience, thoroughly enjoying it for what it is—nothing more, nothing less. Witnessing him in action is a great reminder to try to do the same thing myself: enjoy the surrounds, soak up the fresh air and not get lost in my thoughts. (I recently read an article in which the English comedian Miranda Hart confessed that her dog basically taught her mindfulness too!)

Stanley reminds me to appreciate everything in front of me, but I have also discovered other benefits to regularly being outside. There's something about briskly walking in the fresh air that really lends itself to creativity. Whenever I'm out with Stanley and do allow myself to get busy thinking, my thoughts tend to be positive and productive rather than fraught and narrow. I've had some of my best writing ideas while climbing the hills with Stanley, and I often have to make a note of ideas while I'm out there so I don't forget them later.

Stanley is, without a doubt, the most adorable recovery tool around, a great inspiration, a source of endless love and the perfect motivator to get me out into nature and exercising. What's more, Stanley is not a tool I'm going to ever be able to cross off my list; it's too hard to resist those big, beautiful eyes.

MY TOOLBOX

Recovery community

Sober treats

Mindfulness

Gratitude practice (Three Things)

Regular exercise (walks with Stanley)

'You are actually joined by over a hundred thousand people from around the world'

There's something else on the horizon that's helping to keep me feeling positive. I've been reading about a Mindfulness Summit that starts in just a few days. It's all being done online and, from what I can tell, it's a genuine event (not some two-bit, crackpot internet thing). It's being put together by a young Australian woman who calls herself Mrs. Mindfulness, and I've been to her website and it looks legit. (Plus her name alone has me hooked—anyone who goes by a pseudonym starting with 'Mrs' is fabulous in my book! Ha ha.)

According to her site, Mrs. Mindfulness, whose real name is Melli O'Brien, has gathered over 40 of the world's leading experts on meditation and mindfulness for a series of online interviews, practice sessions and presentations. If I sign up, I'll get to hear from one of them every day for the next month. Like, wow! This has come at the perfect time for me—I almost can't believe it's for real. I read through the instructions and it seems that if I pay I'll get instant, unlimited access to all of the material straight away, or I can do it for no charge by listening to each interview during the 24-hour-period that it is made freely available. I check the list of speakers and am really excited to see Ruby Wax, Dan Harris and Mark Williams there, plus many other big names that I recognise—such as Jon Kabat-Zinn, Joseph Goldstein and Tara Brach—alongside many I don't—Shamash Alidina, Vidyamala Burch and Russ Harris.

Holy moly, this is a veritable mindfulness feast! I get totally jazzed and decide it's just what I need to keep my mindful momentum going after having finished Mark and Danny's book.

I take the plunge and register by filling in my name and email address. I decide to be optimistic and go for the free option, committing myself to listening to each interview within 24 hours. I'm really hoping this intense month-long masterclass will cement the concepts of mindfulness in place for me, and make it even easier to keep living this way. I tell Corin about it and he nods supportively. He's been listening to me attempt to articulate all this mindfulness stuff from the beginning, but even so I'm not sure if he fully realises what major and life-changing work I am doing inside my head right now. Hopefully, if nothing else, he's noticing that I've been a lot calmer and happier lately.

Two days later and Day One of the Mindfulness Summit dawns. It's a Thursday, so after Corin and the boys have left the house I tidy up then sit down to log on to the site. I click on the Day One video and up pops Melli herself. She's all smiles as she says, 'Welcome to the Mindfulness Summit, the not-for-profit online conference teaching you how to practise mindfulness and showing you how mindfulness can change your world from the inside out. Thank you for joining us on this journey. You are actually joined by over a hundred thousand people from around the world.'

Whoa. That's an impressive number! I feel quite excited as I listen to Melli. She describes the summit as an interactive event, and promises that each speaker will be interacting with summit participants in the comments section below each daily video. 'We really look forward to connecting with you,' she says.

The Day One interview is over an hour long and—what do you know?—it's with my buddy Professor Mark Williams. What a treat! It looks like Melli is interviewing him via Skype; the video is a split screen, showing her in what must be her home in Australia, and him in his office in the UK. (I peer at the bookshelf behind his head, trying to see what he is reading. It's hard to tell.) For over an hour, I listen to them discuss mindfulness, and by the end of it I am even more in love with the calm and wise Mark, and even more determined to continue with my mindful ways. Mark's voice is so soothing and gentle, but he's as sharp as a tack, and has a way of talking about life that is really encouraging and inspiring. Melli has a very relaxed and approachable interview manner that makes me feel very connected to them both from my living room in suburban New Zealand. (It's a good thing they can't see me in my old comfy pants and slippers!)

What small thing can I do in the next hour or two that will nourish me?

During the interview, Mark talks about the mental habits we all fall into, and the things we can do to stop ourselves getting caught—things like all the little grounding exercises I've been doing lately to break me out of rumination and worry. He also talks about the tendency we have to get preoccupied with work and other projects to the detriment of doing enjoyable and enriching things in our lives. He says, when we get busy, we promise ourselves that as soon as things calm down we'll do the enjoyable things again—but we never do. The end of one project just signals the start of another, so we never get the chance to give ourselves much nourishment. This is me to a tee! Whenever I have a big writing project on, or Corin heads away overseas, or something comes up that makes my life busier than before, all my self-care habits go out the window (usually the first thing to go is my diet—it turns to shit and becomes very fatty and sugary). It's difficult to break out of that cycle. Mark says:

> We promise ourselves that next year, in the New Year, after this vacation, after this ... then we'll start enjoying the life that we actually promised ourselves. But it actually becomes a bit of a delusion. It never actually happens. So the question

is, how can I nourish myself in the next hour? Not even in the next day but what can I do, some small thing, in the next hour or two that actually will make a difference and give myself a break and give me some practice at attending to my life in a more wholesome way?

I like this concept a whole lot. It reminds me of the sober treats I have enthusiastically embraced since I quit drinking— except that maybe with Mark's 'wholesome' idea in mind I could choose sober treats that aren't always of the fatty or sweet variety. (Note to self: make more green juices and smoothies.) I feel inspired to up my game on the self-care front, and to always try to remember Mark's question: What small thing can I do in the next hour or two that will nourish me?

One of the best things I get from the video is the reassurance that my busy-as-all-hell, wandering mind is not only normal but necessary for practising formal meditations (not that I've done many of them). Mark says a lot of people who begin meditating for the first time think the practice is all about clearing the mind (yep, that's me), and that myth is often perpetrated by images of a monk at the top of a mountain who looks completely blissed out (yep, that was my mental image), whereas what is actually likely to be going through that blissed-out monk's head is the same collection of mundane thoughts I have, such as, *Ow, this stone is a bit hard* or *I feel a bit hungry.*

Given this mistaken perception of what meditation really is, it's no wonder people give up when they first try it! When their mind wanders all over the place, they think they can't do it because that's not what they think should be happening. I've always felt like I was failing at meditation because I could never stop my busy mind for very long to focus on my breath, but now Mark is telling me that my mind wandering is actually vital for the practice; we need the thoughts in order to be able to meditate. He says if I sat down to meditate and my mind didn't wander it would be like going to a gym with no equipment—the thoughts in my mind are the equipment I require to practise the art of identifying and observing my thoughts. This is very reassuring... although I'm afraid it doesn't spur me into doing any more formal sit-down meditations. I just don't want to.

After finishing the video, I get up to make a nourishing mug of chai tea, and while I'm standing waiting for the jug to boil I suddenly decide to be all interactive as they suggested. I quickly get back on to the computer and leave a comment underneath the video. I go full fangirl and type a gushing note:

> Hi—listening from Wellington New Zealand. Loved this first interview—thanks so much, Melli, for all the work you've done in pulling this together. I just adore Mark Williams, having read his book and followed his eight-week course to the letter(!) and have the accompanying audios downloaded on to my phone to

listen to when I need it. Often I drive to school to pick up my kids fifteen minutes early and sit in the car doing one of his guided meditations... a way that I have found to fit meditation in my busy days. Cheers, Lotta.

This is *mostly* true. I have listened to the audios occasionally since the eight-week course ended—although, in all honesty, not that often, but enough that I feel OK claiming to have done so. I feel pretty good leaving the comment, but not as *fantastic* as I feel when, just an hour later, after having done some jobs around the house, I check back and discover that Melli was telling the truth. They *are* interacting with the summit attendees... AND MARK HIMSELF HAS REPLIED TO ME!

Now, I know the world is small and the internet connects us all in brilliant ways and Mark is just a human with a computer like I am, but still this feels like some sort of supernatural magic. Particularly given I have a huge (completely non-romantic, I hasten to add) crush on Mark and he has been inside my head for the past couple of months, changing the way I live. My heart is racing as I read his words.

Thanks, Lotta. I can picture you waiting for your children. What a lovely way to find time to nourish yourself. Many blessings. Mark.

This is, without a shadow of a doubt, the best bit of online feedback I have *ever* received. Mark Williams himself, Professor Mark Williams, the mindfulness guru, talking directly to me online, thinking about me, using my name, picturing me in my car, telling me I have found a lovely way to nourish myself, and wishing me many blessings!

My life is complete.

Chapter 15

'Life sucks, everything changes, don't take it personally'

And so it is on this awesome high that I head forth into the Mindfulness Summit. I am proud of myself for—thanks to Mark's encouraging words (he spoke to *me*!) and to my own positive energy about the event—staying true to my goal to listen to every single speaker every day for the entire month. Some days I listen while lying on the sofa with the iPad propped up on my knees. Some days I sit up at my computer while also doing the odd bit of work, and others (quite a few, actually) I listen while lying on my bed. I am so committed to the summit that I even listen to it for the week we are away on a family holiday in the middle of the month. And, as every day passes with yet another enlightening speaker, I get drawn even more deeply into the fascinating (and wise and kind) world of mindfulness.

Truth be told, I attack the whole event like a super-geek, taking notes as I listen to each speaker and typing up little highlight summaries for my blog about what each of them has to say. Often I visit an expert's website after I've heard them talk, sometimes signing up for their free newsletters, occasionally ordering their books from the online library catalogue. I am going for full immersion, and as a result it feels like I'm doing a fabulous free university course without the added pressure of essays or exams. The only pressure I feel is the pressure I'm putting on myself to absorb every bit of wisdom these experts have to offer.

It's incredible that I am managing to find so much time to devote to the event while also running the house and the kids, plus keeping up with all my online work and reality-TV watching. But, then again, I spent years making time for alcohol—acquiring alcohol, drinking alcohol and recovering from alcohol—and more lately have made time for sobriety—working on getting sober, thinking about not drinking, reading about being in recovery and writing about it every day—so of course I can find the time to devote to being a student of mindfulness.

Really, I'm sure I could find the time to do anything if I was interested and motivated enough in the subject. If I decided knitting was the answer to my happiness, I'm sure I could spend an hour or so every day working on my yarn skills. Or, if I decided to finally give my thighs some love, I'm sure I could find time to train for a marathon (I wish I was motivated to do that!). Right now, it so happens that mindfulness is my obsession, so I am happy to make time for it in my life and I can't believe my luck that someone is running an easily accessible, incredibly enriching and free month-long summit all about it. It's unbelievably great!

I watch as Dan Harris explains why he named his mindfulness book *10% Happier*: 'Sometimes it's sold as quick enlightenment and it's not that at all. My wife thinks I should retitle the book *90% Still A Moron* because it's not solved all of my problems.'

I watch Ruby Wax—all big hair and vulnerability—describe how mindfulness has helped her deal with crippling depression. I hear a lovely, clever guy called Jono Fisher describe how so many of us turn to consumerism to try to improve our lives, when we really need to look at developing ourselves on the inside—not the outside—if we want to feel better.

I listen to a very serious Tami Simon explain that our thinking mind doesn't define our experience.

I really relate to Joseph Goldstein's description of mindfulness as a 'sudden awakening, gradual cultivation'. (Remember he was the one who first introduced me to the concept of thoughts being little energy puffs in the mind?) I've definitely had a sudden awakening to mindfulness (after getting sober, it seems I'm having a sudden awakening to so much!) but I can see that it's going to be a gradual process to cultivate and maintain the practice.

A groovy-looking woman called Timothea Goddard, who has red hair and funky earrings, speaks about how every person is a process, not a problem to be solved or fixed. I like this; it relaxes me, because I can never seem to get away from the idea that if I work hard on myself I will one day 'fix' all my 'problems' and be perfect. Timothea also tells Melli one of the greatest things to come from regularly practising mindfulness is that we become a little less surprised, less shocked, less pained when really difficult things arise in our lives. 'Greed, hatred and ignorance rise endlessly. Also impermanence—old age, death and sickness come to us all.' Then she offers a genius summary of the nature of things: 'Life sucks, everything changes, don't take it personally.' Word, Timothea!

A very trim (of course) clinical psychologist called Susan Albers, who has written six books on the subject of mindful eating, features in one of the videos. I'm very interested in her talk, seeing as my biggest issue since giving up the booze is bingeing on bad food. I watch as she tells Melli she's retrained herself out of comfort eating simply by paying full attention when she's putting food into her mouth. I make a note of her top tip, which is to follow the Five S's when eating: Sit down, smell the food, savour the food, slowly chew, and smile. I try this for half a day and then forget.

I struggle to follow a guy called Elisha Goldstein, because he speaks so fast that I can barely keep up! He's fascinating, though, and in the end I do manage to follow along OK with what he's saying. He describes mindfulness as a 'curious, open, warm awareness' and I'm delighted when he starts talking about the power of the 'informal practice', which is little mindfulness techniques to use in daily life, rather than having to do a formal meditation. This makes me feel so much better about the fact that I'm not doing any sit-down meditations— you know, back straight not rigid, eyes closed, focusing on the breath, noticing thoughts as they arise and bringing the attention back to the breath. He tells Melli that mini moments of 'conscious awareness' can have a real impact on our lives, and that sometimes a regular informal practice can lead to a regular formal practice—and sometimes an informal practice is all you ever do and that's OK too. Well, that's good to hear, because my practice is *very* informal but involves regular moments throughout my day when I remember to stop all the thinking and ground myself in the present moment, by looking at what my hands are doing, or by pausing to feel my breath coming and going.

Some of the summit experts have very specific areas of interest. I listen to people talk about mindful parenting, mindfulness for kids, mindfulness for creativity, mindfulness for dealing with chronic pain, mindfulness for addictions, and—very pertinent for me—mindfulness with technology.

'Experience now; share later'

The summit speaker who focuses her talk almost entirely on how to marry mindfulness with technology is the young, blonde and perky Lori Deschene, who is the founder of the website Tiny Buddha. She is so cute and successful that as I watch her interview I'm hit with a wave of envy about her all-round amazingness. Luckily, I manage to push my green-eyed monster aside (in a mindful fashion of course, which is to say without beating myself up about it!) to focus on her talk because I know I need to do something about the amount of time I spend online. Practical tips are what I want please, Lori. Luckily she has a few.

She says one of the best things she does is to be honest with herself about her intentions when sharing things online. She asks herself whether she's posting purely to get attention or to make herself look good, or whether there's a better, more unselfish reason to share.

I could definitely bear this in mind more often. For the most part, I use my social media accounts to promote alcohol-free living and recovery, and to offer support and encouragement to other sober people, or to people who want to quit drinking but haven't quite got there yet. But if I'm really honest there are probably times when I'm over-sharing simply because I'm bored or because I want more internet love.

She also offers a great mantra to live by, which is 'experience now; share later'. What this means in practice is that you shouldn't upload photos of an event or experience while you're still in the middle of it, because all this does is take you away from fully experiencing the moment itself. By all means, snap a picture with the full intention of sharing it online later— whether it's the delicious mocktail a bartender just made you, or your dog cavorting happily on a walk—but don't share it to social media until later. As Lori points out, when you do share something immediately, you can't help checking who has liked it and commented on it, and in the process you completely miss the moment. This is easily a new internet habit that I could adopt, since I'm totally guilty of uploading photos while I'm out and about and then checking obsessively to see what feedback I'm getting. Not only does this take me away from the actual, real-life moment I'm in, but it's also a bad look and sometimes quite rude! I decide to fully embrace this 'experience now; share later' idea. I'm sure the internet won't notice if I'm a few hours late in sharing my experiences. (Sure enough, as I write this I'm yet to receive angry feedback of the 'how dare you share that photo from two days ago?' variety.)

Another thing Lori talks about is how she's cultivated the confidence to create distance between herself and her devices—for example, she'll often leave her phone down the other end of the house if she's watching a movie with her partner. This gets me thinking. I know I need to do something like this myself, because running my websites and social media accounts from home makes it very difficult for me to get any separation between my work life and my home life. My phone is literally by my side all day and all night. It sits on my bedside table while I sleep. I don't even use it as an alarm clock, so I don't have that excuse.

Other summit speakers bring up the need for those of us with hyper-connected lives to give ourselves a break from time to time. Arianna Huffington makes the humorous (and also sadly true) point that most of us take better care of our smartphones than we do of ourselves—for example, anxiously monitoring their battery life to ensure they don't die on us. This is incredibly foolish, she says, and leads to burnout and exhaustion—we all need downtime, where we unplug our devices to get some space to ground ourselves in the present moment.

After mulling this over for a few days, I come up with a plan—a simple way that I can get a break from my devices. I decide that, from now on, my bedroom will be a device-free zone for me. I will not bring my phone or iPad or laptop down that end of the house. I get busy, moving my chargers away from beside our bed and into the kitchen.

'What are you doing?' Corin asks from his perch at the bench, where he is drinking coffee and scrolling through Twitter.

'No more internet in the bedroom for me,' I announce. 'I'm creating space between me and my devices.'

'Righto,' he says and goes back to his phone.

And so it is that, with the help of the Mindfulness Summit, I adopt a few rules and boundaries with regard to my internet usage. I now never surf the internet in the bedroom. My devices are put on to charge in the kitchen in the early evening, and are left there overnight until I am up and dressed the following morning. I'm sure this new habit has led to me sleeping better; I'm no longer being weirdly stimulated by that electronic blue light right before I nod off. (Many experts say that the light from electronic devices affects levels of the sleep-inducing hormone melatonin.) It has also given me a lovely, gentle start to the day, one where I gently come to consciousness by letting my brain wake slowly, rather than forcing it into concentration mode by instantly reaching for my phone to check what emails have come in overnight and whether I have any feedback on my social media accounts.

At first this habit took a bit of getting used to, but slowly it has become my norm. The longer I live with this boundary in place, the more I realise that there is never any matter so urgent that it can't wait twelve or so hours until I'm ready to address it. There's a real freedom in giving myself this space from the online world, and I feel quite empowered by the knowledge that I've taken ownership of my internet use; I'm not forced into thinking about any online interactions until I'm properly awake, dressed and ready to do so.

Don't get me wrong—I still spend hours and hours and hours online each week, surfing numerous websites, but with some checks and balances in place I really do feel like 'healthy internet habits' is at last a robust tool in my toolbox.

MY TOOLBOX

Recovery community

Sober treats

Mindfulness

Gratitude practice (Three Things)

Regular exercise (walks with Stanley)

Healthy internet habits

My healthy internet habits aren't just limited to the 'no surfing in the bedroom' and 'experience now; share later' rules, either. Since the summit, I've opened up an honest dialogue with myself about the time I spend online, and I constantly keep an eye on it. Sometimes I'll admit to myself that it's getting out of hand (usually when my Internal Observer points out that this is the fourth time in an hour I've checked Facebook) and take steps to limit myself for a while to get some balance back in my life. Lately, for example, I've been experimenting with turning off roaming data on my phone so that when I'm out of the house I can't obsessively check my online spaces. This has been hard! But also quite rewarding—I've actually been reading books while my kids have their swimming lessons! I also recently took a complete break from the internet—a 'cyber holiday' or a 'digital detox' (call it what you will). For seven whole days, while away on holiday with my extended family, I didn't go online *once*! I thought it would be a really big deal, as it took a bit of organising beforehand—among other things, I had to find someone to keep an eye on the Living Sober website while I was away—but in actual fact it was not that dramatic. I had a few urges to check my emails during the week, but it was easy to resist. Overall, I didn't miss going online at all.

In fact, it was an interesting exercise because I noticed throughout the week that the only thing I was really missing and wondering about was what was happening in the world of celebrity gossip (sad but true). Suffice to say, when I got back online and checked the *Daily Mail* website, there was nothing of any interest there other than the obligatory reality-TV star getting drunk and more details about Brad and Angelina's breakup. I made a decision then and there to end my *Daily Mail* addiction and never to visit their website again—and I have stuck to my guns!

Sometimes you just gotta have some mindless fun

During the final week of the Mindfulness Summit, I get a text from my friend reminding me that we have committed to trying a different yoga class at the rec centre. *Tonight's the night for yoga!* her text reads. Incredibly, when I see her words, I don't do my usual inward groan; instead I find myself strangely open to the idea of giving yoga another go. Maybe it's because I'm fully immersed in a world of depth and meaning right now, listening to wise sages speak on the topic of mindfulness every day. Or maybe it's because the kids are doing my head in and I want an evening off.

I type out *Sounds good*, but before pressing send I get sidetracked and spend ages looking for an appropriate yoga-based emoji. Sadly, I can see no downward-dog icons on my phone's emoji keyboard, so I go to the app store and download Kim Kardashian's Kimoji app in the hopes she has something I can use. Does she what! I decide a twerking Kimoji isn't really appropriate, but there is one of her doing a handstand that would fit with the yoga theme of my text. I add it in and send it. Fun! I decide to spend some more time sending friends random Kimojis, just for laughs. I send one friend the twerking Kimoji. My sister gets a big-boobs Kimoji. Corin gets a pole-dancing Kimoji. This whole process takes at least fifteen minutes and I'm sure it's not very mindful but it certainly is fun. I'm very aware of what I am doing, though, so you could say I'm mindfully using technology to connect with my friends—or you could say I'm wasting time online, avoiding the present moment. Take your pick. Sometimes you just gotta have some mindless fun.

Later that evening, as the yoga class approaches, I get ready by once again putting on my mum's hand-me-down stripy leggings, but I think smart for once and put on a tighter-fitting T-shirt that shouldn't expose my breasts to the world if I have to hang upside down. As soon as Corin gets home, I practically bolt out of the door, throwing a quick 'Don't let the boys stay up late!' behind me as I depart. I drive to the rec centre (mindfulness hasn't cured me of all my lazy tendencies) and meet my friend out the front as arranged. Together we make our way past the waddling pregnant ladies who are heading to an antenatal class with their protective partners, past the sweaty teenagers playing basketball noisily in the main gym, and up the stairs into a small back room where our class is being held. I'm nervous and out of my comfort zone as I head into this bendy and flexible environment, but I'm feeling slightly more positive than ever before.

This is my final go at giving yoga a shot.

Chapter 16

Who knew that yoga could be about having fun?

The moment I walk through the door, I sense this is a different atmosphere to any yoga class I've ever been in. First off, it's a really small room with floor-to-ceiling windows along one side, which makes it lovely and light. Second, there's a relaxed and bubbly hum of chatter going on. It sounds more like a cruisy afternoon tea than a serious yoga class (but without the cakes, sadly). There are about seven people lying around casually on their mats. I turn to the front and am amazed to see that I recognise the instructor—our sons used to play on the same rugby team! She's mid-laugh in conversation with someone but catches my eye and says a cheery, 'Hey, you!'

'Hey!' I reply (battling to remember her name—I am crap at remembering names). I instantly feel a little more relaxed about what's ahead. My friend and I head over to the corner to take our coats and shoes off and lay out our mats.

A short time later what's-her-name starts the class. I work out pretty quickly that (unlike my previous, unpleasant forays into yoga) I'm not in for a hellish hour of uptightness this time. This yoga instructor (whose name I'm later reminded is Nicola) is all about being relaxed, friendly and—amazingly!—having fun. Who knew that yoga could be about having fun? In this class I discover that it can. There is joking and banter throughout, and remarkably I find myself really enjoying it.

For the next hour, we bend and stretch and twist and hang, but it's all done at a very relaxed pace and with clear instructions. I think that's one of the key things for me here: the instructions are very easy to follow, and Nicola keeps giving us options so that we can choose whether or not to do the more advanced version of each pose. She keeps saying things like, 'If this is too much, then drop down to your knees,' or, 'This bit is an optional add-on—you are welcome to just stay where you are for now.' At one point she even says, 'Don't do this if you don't want to. You can just stay lying comfortably on your back for now.'

Thanks, Nicola, I will!

It's unbelievable how comfortable I feel in her class. There is no pressure for me to perform in any particular way. I don't feel bad that my chest doesn't touch my thighs when I do a forward bend. I don't feel bad that I choose not to rotate my plank pose. I don't feel bad that I come out of my downward dog early because my upper arms are killing me. I just go at the pace that suits me right now, and that's perfectly OK.

The class winds down in the usual way, with us all lying in the 'corpse pose' while Nicola guides us in a relaxation. I'd be lying if I didn't admit that I spend some of my 'corpse' time locked in a fierce internal battle about whether or not to buy myself some chocolate on the way home—but it is a mindful battle, in the sense that I can see what I am doing. My Internal Observer has a disapproving eye on me (she isn't happy about the chocolate debate) and after a short while she helps me to focus on my breath. Once I quit obsessing about sugar and start listening to Nicola's calming words, I begin to really appreciate being in a room with other humans, doing what is basically a guided meditation. I am in a heightened mindful state right now, and I find it's actually lovely to be doing this. Super lovely!

I feel so good that, when the class ends, I whisper to my friend, 'That was great! We should come again!'

She nods in agreement, and with that a firm habit is formed. (I am also proud to say I didn't buy any chocolate on the way home that night, either.) I am now in my sixth straight term of attending Tuesday-night yoga classes at my local rec centre.

Amazingly, for me, it is no longer a chore getting there. I don't spend my entire Tuesday trying to talk myself out of it, nor do I clock-watch during the class, waiting for it to end. I look forward to going, thoroughly enjoy it while I'm there, and feel excellent afterwards. In actual fact, I feel excellent for the *entire week* afterwards! I am so dedicated that, whenever Corin is away travelling for work, I hire a babysitter to look after the boys so I can attend.

Sometimes I find it hard to explain exactly what it is I love about my yoga class so much. It seems crazy that doing something for only one hour out of an entire week can have such a positive impact on my whole experience of life, but, believe me, it does. It puts me in touch with my body in a way that nothing else in my life ever has before. Given I have spent most of my life being very out of touch with my body, this is a remarkable feeling. For one hour every week, Nicola guides me in a series of poses and exercises that I thoroughly enjoy. She makes my body bend and stretch in ways that it wouldn't otherwise in the normal course of my days. Sure, I have an active life, running around after my kids, but I do also spend a lot of time sitting down—driving the car, or at my keyboard—so being forced to do back bends and twisty turns feels great.

I truly have become a yoga convert. Yes, it's true. It really has happened. I have become a complete and utter yoga convert. Not in a look-at-me-do-handstands-under-a-waterfall kind of way (I am still decidedly un-sporty, have a very wobbly tummy, and can't achieve the most flexible poses), but I don't care. I just feel great about doing it and so happy to have it in my life. It took me three attempts to find a teacher with the vibe that suited me personally (chatty and relaxed), and I'm so glad I persevered. I also don't think it's a coincidence that I've finally taken to yoga at a time in my life when I am working on connecting more deeply with myself and the world around me. Yoga fits into my new lifestyle brilliantly. It feels nourishing and kind, and I intend to keep doing it for a very long time. Yoga has become a fantastic tool in my toolbox.

MY TOOLBOX

Recovery community

Sober treats

Mindfulness

Gratitude practice (Three Things)

Regular exercise (walks with Stanley)

Healthy internet habits

Yoga

If I could achieve this then I really would be a truly Zen housewife

The Mindfulness Summit is still going, and in everything I watch and hear two big, overarching themes start to emerge. The first is compassion.

When I first hear the word 'compassion' being thrown about by various experts, I'm not entirely sure what exactly they mean (or how it plays out in practicality), but as the days go on I start to get a clearer idea. A silver-haired and healthy-looking expert called Jack Kornfield has a great line about how compassion is vital to mindfulness. He tells Melli that the goal of mindfulness isn't to become some sort of uptight and rigid mindful person, but to become fluid (and there's *that* word again). He says the aim isn't to be perfect, but to perfect your ability to be present, open-hearted and compassionate. I want to walk through the world with a compassionate heart. Like, all the time. No matter how many dicks I come across. If I could achieve this, then I really would be a truly Zen housewife.

Another healthy-looking dude (come to think of it, all of the summit speakers are healthy-looking—bet none of them have sugar binges) called Shamash Alidina, the very chirpy author of *Mindfulness for Dummies*, also emphasises the importance of having a kind and compassionate mindset. He says mindfulness is about more than just being present and paying attention to the here and now; what also matters is the *way* in which you pay attention. He calls this having the right 'mindful attitude'—one full of kindness, warmth, affection and friendliness. He says you should never criticise yourself for any negative thoughts or for your mind wandering, and that you should be kind to yourself always. 'If you had a good friend that kept rabbiting on about stuff on their mind, you wouldn't get grumpy with them, you'd be kind. You should be the same about your own wandering mind.'

And my special friend Mark Williams agrees (we've interacted directly now so I feel confident elevating our friendship to the level of 'special'): 'Many mindfulness teachers are very aware their mind wanders all the time. And as you get more and more practice, it's not that your mind doesn't wander; it's that there's an ease of returning, a sense of self-forgiveness, a sense of cultivating compassion for yourself.'

There's one thing in particular that Shamash says about compassion that I find really helpful. I've been thinking a lot lately that just dropping my tricky thoughts in order to focus on the clouds isn't a good enough tool on its own to help me deal with stuff. In fact, it could be seen as an avoidance technique, and we all know where that has got me in the past (hello, booze habit). Shamash tells me that I should use my kind and compassionate mindset to lean *into* unpleasant feelings and examine them. He says it's OK to focus on the negative thoughts sometimes, so long as it's done with that 'mindful attitude' of compassion, warmth and kindness. He wisely points out that often our immediate reaction to a negative thought is to think, *Oh no, I don't want to have that thought*, then try to either push it away or bury it. But, as we all know, these negative thoughts have a nasty habit of bouncing right back at you, usually when they're least helpful. If you try to bring a compassionate, friendly attitude to your negative thoughts, he suggests, they'll often seem to soften and eventually dissolve.

Joseph Goldstein also talks about the importance of fostering an interest in what is happening to you at any given time. He calls it 'awakening into compassion', and explains that being interested in what's going on in your mind and body—whether it's awesome or awful—can lead to understanding. I guess that's what people mean when they say, 'What doesn't break you makes you stronger.'

'If we are interested in what's happening—whether it's a wonderful state of mind or a difficult one—if we are interested then it really leads to understanding. And very often it's the times of the greatest suffering that lead to the greatest insight.'

I like the idea that if I can stay kind and compassionate towards myself during life's tough times, and also open and interested about what is going on for me, then I'll learn and grow. Even better, it seems the experts are telling me that if I apply compassion to myself regularly, then it will start to radiate out to others. I listen to Jack Kornfield tell me that, when you start to live, act and respond to life more mindfully and compassionately, it starts to have an effect on the people around you and they feed off that. That sounds great. I think I can do that.

'Compassion is not a soft option. It is an act of courage'

One of the summit experts, a clinical psychologist called Paul Gilbert, is so into compassion that his presentation is actually called 'The Importance of Self-compassion'. He is super smart and has such a great way of explaining the human brain and life on earth and the difficulties that all of us face. I find listening to him really reassuring and empowering. One of the things he mentions is how important it is to remind yourself that, no matter what's going on or what's happening to you, it's not your fault. You don't get to choose the brain you're born with, and working out how to manage your mind isn't necessarily something that comes naturally, so you shouldn't beat yourself up about it. *That's like what Ruby said about our Ferrari brains that no one gave us the keys to!* I think.

Paul speaks for ages and it's all so bloody interesting that I am absolutely riveted to the screen. (I'm lying in bed watching on the iPad while eating tomatoes on toast for this one.) He helps me to really understand how bringing an attitude of kindness and compassion to myself and my own busy (and sometimes negative) mind will help that attitude radiate out to the people around me: And then he hits me with the awesomely rousing statement: 'Compassion is not a soft option. It is an act of courage.' I like this challenge. Bring it on!

This notion of compassion is one of the best things to come out of the summit for me. It's helping me to grow a real sense of connectedness with my fellow humans that I find very calming. I know this sounds quite Pollyanna-ish, but it's true. This sense of togetherness started growing for me right back when I first began to connect with other people who struggled with alcohol addiction, and it has been expanding to include all humans since my exploration of mindfulness started—for example, Ruby got me thinking about all of the blobs of play dough in our heads, and my doctor about all the other teary patients she sees. And now all these summit experts are ramming home the same message: I am not alone in my struggles with my emotions and moods, nor am I weak or unusual for having them. One by one, these experts are validating the truth that life is bloody hard for all of us, with our busy brains and our tricky emotions and the seemingly endless stream of bad and hurtful stuff that happens. Paul Gilbert puts it pretty bluntly when he says:

> Life is actually really quite hard. The reality check is the fact that all of us have been created by our genes. Having genes

that build our bodies means that we have two arms and legs and eyes because genes build them. We also have a brain that our genes have built. In this brain we have capacities for all kinds of motivations and emotions. We have the capacities for anger, for anxiety, for lust, for joy, and of course also for compassion. We have to figure out how to work with all these different impulses, feelings, going on inside of us.

I love the idea of elevating compassion to a higher status. It just feels bloody nice to have compassion for myself and for others. This concept is so entrenched in my mind now that I'd even go so far as to say it is its own powerful tool in my toolbox.

MY TOOLBOX

Recovery community

Sober treats

Mindfulness

Gratitude practice (Three Things)

Regular exercise (walks with Stanley)

Healthy internet habits

Yoga

Compassion

First and foremost, I turn my compassion on myself, because I now know that if I am kind and loving and forgiving to myself then I am better placed to spread those feelings out to those around me. So I think kindly about myself when I go through a glum phase, and tell myself that it's OK to be feeling low, that it's normal and that it will pass. I forgive myself constantly for binging on sugar when I'm stressed out or in a funk, and I tell myself that nobody's perfect and sugar is a really hard addiction to beat (and I remind myself that at least I don't touch alcohol, ever). I forgive myself for snapping at the kids when I'm tired and short-tempered, and I tell myself that no mother of three boisterous sons is perfectly calm all the time. I forgive myself for having a messy week during which I feel teary or antisocial, and I tell myself that tears are little messages from the soul and it's OK to hibernate and cry sometimes. I forgive myself for the times when I forget to be mindful and instead get lost in my thoughts, and I remind myself that I have a Ferrari brain, which is hard to manage, and that it's understandable if it sometimes gets stuck on autopilot. I forgive myself for forming unkind or judgemental thoughts, and I tell myself that they are just little energy puffs born from environmental factors like tiredness or insecurity, and that they don't mean I'm an unkind or judgemental person.

In other words, I forgive myself constantly for being an ordinary, messy, imperfect human being. Simply by doing this—by turning compassion on myself—I feel a little better day in, day out. Like many of the tools in my toolbox, compassion is something that has a subtle and slow impact. The strength of the practice isn't in the individual moments when I use it, but in the cumulative effect of having it as a regular feature in my life.

Compassion also has far more of a benefit than just making me feel better about myself; it also works to combat phases when I'm getting too self-absorbed, by taking me out of myself. By kindly reminding myself that I'm imperfect and that's OK, I find it impossible not to think kindly towards other people in the same way. So this is how compassion starts to radiate out to the people around me—just like the experts said it would!

I try to look kindly upon everyone now. We're all in the same boat. We're all imperfect humans trying desperately to navigate our Ferrari minds. We're all dealing with moods and emotions and complications and pain. We all have good days and bad days, glum phases and egotistical phases. We all get stuck on autopilot sometimes, or led by our thoughts as though they are gospel and must be adhered to strictly. I find it incredibly calming to look at another person and know that I can't even begin to imagine the complicated dialogue they have going on inside their own head. I don't need to know the details; just reminding myself that they've probably got as much going on as I have helps. This compassionate way of looking at others helps me massively if I try to do it on a regular basis.

Chapter 17

'History has delivered us this moment'

The second big concept that emerges for me during the summit is acceptance. A simple word that implies a hugely important mindset. It's pretty self-explanatory: accept everything that happens, because it's a waste of time to wish it hadn't. This is a big one for me, because I don't think I've ever been very good at this—I tend to spend a lot of time wishing bad situations away, wishing that things were different, and as a result I add an extra layer of angst to already hard times. When my beloved step-father was dying, a huge part of my mind during that time of grief was taken up with wishing that he wasn't sick, wishing

232

that he wasn't leaving us, wishing that things weren't the way they were.

I wonder if my sadness and pain might have been lessened, even a teeny tiny bit, if I had been more accepting of the situation? According to a guy called Michael Chaskalson, the founder of an outfit called Mindfulness Works Ltd. and one of the summit experts, it would have. He says acceptance (which he calls the 'wisdom element' of mindfulness) 'entails choosing to allow what is the case to be the case. It's surprising how much energy we all put into *not* allowing what is the case be the case. We wish it were "not like this", "they shouldn't do this", "it shouldn't be like that", "why has this turned up now?" But you know what? What's here is just what's here. What's shown up has shown up. History has delivered us this moment and it couldn't be anything other than it is. It is what it is. And when we can allow that it is what it is, then we begin to have some choice.' I like this mantra 'history has delivered us this moment'. I find it very calming.

Joseph Goldstein calls acceptance the 'freeing aspect' of mindfulness, and says it's the aspect that allows things to pass through our lives with more ease. Russ Harris tells Melli that the important thing is that 'there's an attitude of openness to what is here right now. I might not like it. I might not want it. I might not approve of it, but I'm open to it. I'm not fighting with it. I'm not running away from it. I'm open to it.'

I get to thinking more and more about acceptance as the summit goes on, and realise I first got a whiff of the concept when I worked through my issue with that other mum after the playdate incident (the non-issue, I should say, which I unnecessarily built up into World War III in my mind). That process had me consciously letting go of the issue, rather than continuing to overwork it in my mind, and it worked a treat—I really was able to drop all of my internal angst about her. But now, listening to the summit, I'm starting to see that acceptance is about more than just letting go; it's about allowing everything that comes along to be just as it is. I need to simply accept it for what it is (there really isn't another word to describe acceptance other than acceptance).

What acceptance *doesn't* mean is that I'm choosing to like negative events, agree with dickheads or take unfair crap; all it means is that I'm not wasting my energy on wishing those things didn't exist. First and foremost, I'm accepting them for what they are. It's quite a radical notion, when you think about it, because it almost runs counter to our natural reaction, which is to hope for things to remain smooth and easy and calm all the time. But, even though we all know deep down that life is hard and shit happens, it's still unusual and radical (well, it is to me, thus far in my life anyway) to accept the bad stuff when it comes along.

I decide to apply this acceptance theory to a current situation in my life: the colleague who I am finding it tricky to work with. (Yep, I am still having trouble in that department.) I work on dropping the internal dialogue that wishes that the situation was different. Instead, I try to relax and accept that, for better or worse and whether I like it or not, things are the way they are, and I can't control the behaviour of others. It's a subtle mind-shift for me, but slowly and amazingly I do start to feel more relaxed about them. I *accept* them. I feel less hard done by every time we interact, and less wound up during the silent times in between our interactions (which is usually the time when I would get extremely angsty and have imaginary heated discussions with them). This subtle yet positive change in my mindset comes about even though nothing external has changed. All that has shifted is my thinking, and due to that I am calmer about the whole relationship. This truly is remarkable. Once more, I'm discovering that if I simply change how I think about things they will improve, even if nothing changes in real life.

Right now, today, is the only moment I've actually got to live

As time has gone on since the summit, I've practised bringing a measure of acceptance to everything that happens (rather than waste my time wishing it away). I've noticed that I feel calmer in times of stress. I'm now better placed in the heat of any given moment to make decent decisions about how to act, so long as I choose first and foremost to accept things for what they are. If I can remember to consciously think, *History has delivered me this moment. It is what it is. Now what am I going to do about it?* rather than, *This sucks! I wish it wasn't happening!* then I find a slight edge is taken off and I'm more open, flexible and willing to deal with it. Pausing and remembering to breathe and respond, rather than react, helps too.

So, when we're decorating the Christmas tree and, instead of it being a lovely family time, our kids are fighting and hitting each other, I don't waste energy thinking, *It's outrageous that they're acting this way. They're ruining the ritual!* Rather, I accept that they're squabbling and think, *How can I best navigate this so they get through the next hour without killing each other?* And when I deal with constant pain due to my Raynaud's syndrome (a circulation problem that causes painful cold attacks) I don't waste time thinking, *I wish I didn't have this condition. Poor me. Woe is me.* Instead I accept that I do have it and think, *This is my thing to deal with. How am I going to manage it so I avoid attacks, and how am I going to deal with them when they come?*

This acceptance concept, along with compassion, is one of the best things to come out of the summit for me. I totally dig it; it has a nice 'go with the flow' edge to it, combined with a pinch of 'it is what it is'. It's simple, but also huge. Since adopting it as a tool and understanding how to use it, it has made a subtle but significant difference to my whole experience of life. It also makes me feel a bit more calm about the future and better prepared for what's to come. I'm allowing more space inside myself to admit that painful and tricky events are going to come along, and I'm prepared to accept them (even if I know they're going to hurt like crazy and be hard to navigate). Thanks to the overall concept of mindfulness, I don't get stuck on worrying about all the bad stuff ahead. With acceptance, I can be prepared to open up to them when they happen, and with mindfulness I can deal with the here and now. Because right now, today, is the only moment I've actually got to live.

MY TOOLBOX

Recovery community

Sober treats

Mindfulness

Gratitude practice (Three Things)

Regular exercise (walks with Stanley)

Healthy internet habits

Yoga

Compassion

Acceptance

By the time the summit ends, I'm feeling relaxed about life and full of positive vibes, fantastic ideas and good intentions. I'm also (if I'm brutally honest) ready to take a break from all the intense self-help discussions, note-taking and blogging about it all. I've been fully immersed and, while it has been the life-changing masterclass I was hoping for, I'm also keen to get some time back into my days.

It's been grand, though—I do feel as though I've been part of something really big and exciting, and I'm determined to use all that I have learned in my continued aim to live life as an uber-calm, Zen, perfectly perfect housewife. Or if not that then at least I'll try my very best to be calm, Zen, mindful and accepting of all things, and kindly forgive myself when I'm not.

I hear one of my favourite quotes from the entire event on the last day, when Mr Cool-Surname, Jon Kabat-Zinn, says:

> Mindfulness is not about bettering yourself; it's about knowing yourself more fully. It doesn't immunise you against bad feelings—you are not trying to achieve some special state. It's just about being with things as they are. It's not always easy, because we don't like bad feelings, but with a compassionate approach we can accept.

Those daffodils are AMAAAAAZING

Not only has the summit given me a bunch of new tools and a greater understanding of my mind, but I've also come away from it finally knowing what the difference is between meditation and mindfulness. Mindfulness exercises are like bicep curls and sit-ups, and can be practised sporadically throughout the day—for example, when I'm driving in the car and realise I'm lost in thought, I'll pull my attention back by concentrating on feeling the vibrations of the steering wheel under my hands. Meditation is like going to the gym to do a concentrated burst of exercise for a set period of time—for example, I meditate by sitting up straight, closing my eyes, recognising thoughts as they pass through, and dropping them to bring my attention back to the sensations of my breath and body. Just as Andy from Headspace said, in fact; he obviously knows what he's on about. From what I have gathered the idea is that if you do the gym workout (in other words, meditate) regularly then you strengthen your brain muscles, making it easier to bring mindfulness to various points throughout your day.

I had grand intentions of developing a regular formal meditation practice (setting the alarm to get up and sit quietly every morning) but, sadly, I haven't managed to do this yet. I like the idea of being a regular meditator, and always admire (and envy) people who are, but for me it's been unachievable so far. As I write this it's a year since the summit, and I've probably only done a dozen or so formal meditations. They never last for very long, I don't feel like I get much out of them, and I never feel highly motivated to rush back into doing it again. I did actually try formally meditating once more when I began writing this book, thinking it would be awesome to end the book by writing about what a clever meditator I had become, and how it was a fantastic part of my life. I told myself, *All I'm doing is sitting down to see what is going on inside my head. Nothing more. No lofty ideals or grand aims. Just sit and see what is going on and remember to bring the attention back to the breath.*

And so I did that. One day, I did it for about two minutes. The next day, I did it for about eight or nine minutes. Both times it went like it always does: noisy and complicated up there at first, then things calmed a little and I started to see clearly defined thoughts more easily and I remembered to keep bringing my attention back to the breath. *Bicep curls for the brain*, I tell myself. *Bicep curls for the brain.* But that was all I did. Twice, and then never again. So the truth remains that for me right now formally meditating just isn't something I can (or want to) do.

I'm sure somebody clever could help me push through my resistance to meditating so that it becomes a regular habit and a wonderfully helpful part of my life (in the way that all those who do it say it is). Or maybe one day things will change for me in such a way that I become desperate for a regular 'time-out' to work on releasing my thoughts. Never say never. Life is long, and I know I've still got a bunch of big, tricky things coming my way that are going to hurt like hell. Maybe when the going gets really rough, I'll take my practice to the next level and formally meditate regularly.

It's good to have that next level up my sleeve if I need to turn to it, but in the meantime I'm OK with what I do have, which is a very solid and robust informal mindfulness practice. I may not be 'going to the gym' by doing formal meditations, but I am 'exercising regularly' by practising the mindfulness techniques I have learned and trying to bring compassion and acceptance to everything I do. And I have discovered that the more I do it, the easier it is to do. It's no exaggeration to say that mindfulness really has transformed my life hugely. For the first time, I am understanding and adopting the 'I am not my thoughts' attitude—and it's liberating!

I feel as though I've undergone a crash course in the reality of the human experience and of my busy brain, and I've woken up to the control I have over how to shape my experience of life. Awakening to what my mind is capable of in the two years since I set this new project in motion has been immense. I am much more aware of the essentially hollow nature of thoughts—that they are not always to be taken as gospel, and that I should hesitate before letting them control my day. As a result, I am far less inclined to get swept up in endless negative-thinking loops. My Internal Observer is a permanent fixture in the corner of my mind, and as a result I'm much, much better at noticing my thoughts without getting lost in them, swayed by them or letting them dominate my whole life experience. Before this self-improvement project began, I was all too often letting my busy and oh-so-clever frontal cortex dominate—always letting my thoughts, plans, ideas, fears, worries, ruminations and memories take the wheel and control my days. But now I understand that I have a choice whether or not to do that. I have experienced the huge benefit there is to be found in switching off (or at least turning the volume down on) that part of my brain and letting the other parts lead—the gentle, sensory parts.

I now have many, many mindful moments throughout the day, when I remind myself to pull away from my thoughts and back into the present moment—to look at the things around me, listen to the sounds, sense the rhythms in my body, feel my breath. I'm more likely now to quietly pause for a good few moments to really savour a flavour, or to appreciate the feeling of the hot sun on my skin or of the raindrops on my head. I'm also far more likely to pause for a good few moments and notice things around me—to let my eyes take in the sights, and to marvel at them without attaching stories to them or being lost elsewhere in thought. I do this quite consciously and deliberately. *Those daffodils are AMAAAAAZING!* I'll think as I wonder at how such a common flower can be so delicate and spectacular. Or I'll be out and about with friends or family and will inwardly and privately think, *Look at all of us, sitting around in a cafe, enjoying each other's company.*

It's like taking a little mental step back to really notice things in a slightly awed way—and doing this regularly makes a huge and lovely difference to my whole experience of life! So simple, yet so effective.

Chapter 18

Practising mindfulness is the ultimate act of self-care

Here's an example of how mindfulness positively impacts my days. Recently, I had a ridiculously crazy day where I ran around like a headless chicken from dawn to dusk: I spent an hour with Mr Seven at the dentist (not fun), collected my mum from the airport, and took Mr Twelve and Mr Ten to their multiple after-school activities. I was trying to fit in some time writing this book (because the deadline was looming), and I was also trying not to worry about Mr D, who was smack-bang in the midst of the heightened scenes in New York in the wake of Donald Trump's election. I barely sat down all day, and was in and out of the house *seven* times (and that's a lot, given there are 39 steps to climb from our house to the garage!). Plus it was pouring with rain all day. My heart was racing and my adrenaline was pumping. It really was a crazy-busy day.

And, on top of all of the busyness, my brain decided to make matters worse. As the day went on, my thoughts got more and more wound up and unhelpful. Pitiful little energy puffs in the form of *Poor me, I'm so tired, I'm working so hard*, and *Does anyone even appreciate what I'm doing?* came flying in, along with the extremely logical, *Mr D might get shot at the protest!*

Yes, my day was busy, and there was a lot going on—but here I was adding a whole extra layer of angst on top of all the activity by thinking negatively about it. However, now that I have my foxy Internal Observer keeping an eye on me, I was able to recognise when things were mentally getting out of hand and to calm myself by using my mindfulness tools. This is not rocket science. It was just a matter of recognising what my thoughts were doing and taking steps to stop them— and therefore avoiding adding that unnecessary extra layer of stress. As I've heard Dan Harris say, 'There's a difference between the raw sensations we experience and the mental spinning we do in reaction to said stimuli.'

So, on this busy day, I made myself focus regularly on my breath. As I climbed the steps to the garage yet again, I stopped the *Woe is me, I'm so tired* thoughts that were creeping in and instead concentrated on the rise and fall of my chest as I breathed. As I stood in the Scout Den waiting for the Cubs meeting to end, I dropped my internal moaning about how long flag break was taking, and instead wriggled my toes and focused on the sensations there. Driving in the car, I noticed that my shoulders were tense and I made myself relax them and concentrate on the feeling of the steering wheel's vibrations under my hands. Standing at the kitchen bench serving dinner, I caught myself worrying about why Corin hadn't texted me back (catastrophising to the extent that I had the police knocking on the door to tell me my husband had been shot), so I forced those thoughts to stop and instead made myself feel the cool air as it entered my nostrils and the warm air as it exited my mouth. And, because I did these simple yet effective things all day (especially between three in the afternoon and nine at night) I didn't end up as an emotional wreck, feeling negative and sorry for myself. Instead, I felt calm and content. Utterly exhausted, yes—but not emotionally low. (And thankfully the protests in New York didn't amount to much, and Corin made it out in one piece.)

These mindfulness techniques might sound ridiculously simple. Seriously, just feeling the vibrations of the steering wheel makes a difference? Yes, it really does. It's not so much about the steering wheel or my breath or the sensations in my toes—those are just readily available grounding tools. It's about recognising the actions of my thinking mind and not being sucked in by them. It's about awareness, and most importantly it's about kindness.

Practising mindfulness is the ultimate act of self-care. I care that I don't get wound up. I care that I don't have butterflies in my tummy. I care that I don't make a busy day worse by thinking negatively about it. And in return all the people around me benefit, and I feel like I'm connecting with them more intensely. After my busy day last week, I ended up having a lovely chat with each of my boys, really connecting with them as I tucked them into bed. I wasn't consumed by my thoughts about how busy I'd been, and there was no tension radiating from me into my sons (and no wine fumes coming out of my mouth, either, as once would have been the case).

This happens a lot now that I am living more mindfully. I feel so much more present in my kids' childhoods, aware that they will be grown up and gone before I know it and I will miss this time with them when they're young. I'm not going to look back and feel like I didn't appreciate their early years, because I keep having little moments inside myself where I pause and really notice them.

Also, since I've begun thinking so often about my breath, I've become very connected to the whole of myself in a wonderful, subtle way. There's something about focusing on this vital bodily action that is incredibly enriching, and noticing it regularly has fostered in me a deeper level of self-love. This is not the same as me looking in the mirror and thinking, *Boy, do I look shit-hot today!* or seeing myself being mentioned online and thinking, *I am so clever!* Actually, it's not about thinking about myself at all. It's about feeling myself—and, as someone who has never really been connected to their physical self at all (how could I be when I was all noise and booze?), slowing down and focusing on my breath regularly has led to me settling and becoming very connected with the whole of myself.

A lot of it comes down to me realising this: I am not my thoughts.

I am *way* more than my thoughts. I am my heart and my soul and the blood pumping in my veins and a miraculous collection of atoms and molecules that takes up space on this earth. My thoughts, on the other hand, are little energy puffs created out of the restless frontal cortex of my mind. They are influenced by the current state I am in, and are often not factual. If I'm tired, I think more negatively. If I'm sick, I think more negatively. If something tricky is going on, I think more negatively.

There are no downsides

For the first time in my life, I am able to separate out my thinking mind from the rest of me, to recognise when it is dominating, and to get it to *just stop*. This is my simple little mindfulness mantra, and it repeats itself often in my mind. It comes to me in a voice that is kind and wise—it's my foxy Internal Observer!—and she says, 'Just stop.'

Just stop with all the mental habits that are winding you up.

Just stop with all the worrying about your life, other people's lives, life in general.

Just stop with all the ruminating over how things should or shouldn't be.

Just stop with all the thinking about yourself that you do.

Just stop with all the planning about how things should be in the future.

Just stop with all the judgement about what's going on.

Just stop with all the comparing yourself to others.

Just stop with all the speculating about what other people are thinking.

Just stop with all the endless mind-chatter.

Just stop.

Of course, I still do all of the above—who doesn't?—but if I catch myself letting it go on for too long I think, *Just stop*, and some sort of switch gets flicked in my mind. I relax my thinking into focusing on what is actually happening right in front of me in the exact moment I'm in.

This is mindfulness! Paying attention to the moment without being lost in my head.

The freedom—the *freedom*—when I practise this regularly is

so great. It's like being able to push a CALM button in my brain so that everything turns lovely. And there are no downsides. Practising mindfulness hasn't led to me forgetting things or mismanaging things or underperforming at things. On the contrary, it's loosened me up overall so that I can perform better when I do need to focus on tasks.

Mindfulness has turned out to be the magic ticket I was looking for.

I often say to people, 'Mindfulness is the answer to everything,' because I genuinely believe it is. For me, mindfulness solves the problem of how to navigate being a human with a busy brain and messy range of emotions who is living a life full of wonders and pain.

I have undergone huge personal growth in the past five and a bit years since I quit drinking, and in particular during the last two years since I launched my new mindfulness project to 'go within' and figure out ways to manage myself emotionally. I've worked hard, researched thoroughly, soaked up knowledge and opened myself up to some wonderful new techniques that are subtle yet powerful and effective. I now have a toolbox *full* of genuine and authentic tools that help me massively in stressful or painful times.

And these tools really work. They have been put to the test lately, as we've been living through a very stressful and anxious time. The region we live in has been hit by some strong and very destructive earthquakes. It's been scary, to say the least. Lives have been lost, highways blocked by slips, houses destroyed and schools closed. Our own property was affected—cracks appeared in the concrete pylons holding up our garage, which doesn't sound like much, except that our house is on a hill (remember the 39 steps!) and the garage juts out directly above our bedroom. We had to get civil engineers in to carry out safety assessments, and it was an anxious month-long wait before they had time to visit (since they were busy checking all the high-rise buildings in town).

I've been unnerved by all of it. Earthquakes are scary and unpredictable, and they've seriously rocked my sense of security. My adrenaline pumps with every aftershock, and my heart drops with every media report telling us that more shocks are likely. And I'm not alone. All my friends around the neighbourhood are sharing stories of broken sleep, kids having panic attacks and frantic shopping trips to stock up on emergency supplies. We are all on edge and looking for ways to cope with the stress. For many (judging by my social media feeds) booze has been a go-to helper, but obviously that is not an option for me anymore. Instead, I have leaned heavily on the tools and techniques I have in my toolbox.

I practised mindfulness. My Internal Observer didn't let any thoughts of being crushed to death take hold. I remembered to use my breath, the sensations of my body, and the sights before my eyes to stop the unnecessary rumination about 'what might be' and instead stay in the moment. Acceptance has helped—accepting that earthquakes are a fact of life on Planet Earth and therefore wishing them away is a waste of time and energy. Instead of pushing my fears away by numbing and avoiding them, I've been moving towards them, acknowledging them with kindness and understanding. Remembering to use compassion and be kind towards myself and others has also helped. I've been reminding myself that all of the people living in my region are probably feeling the same way, and that has helped me broaden my awareness outside of myself. All of these things have helped to ground me, calm me and allow me to continue on.

Continuing on has involved walking Stanley, going to yoga, doing Three Things at night with my kids, making sure I don't spend too long on the internet, buying myself treats like magazines and fresh flowers, and staying in touch with my awesome recovery community. With all of these tools to draw on, I have been able to care for myself in this time of earthquake stress and avoid feeling too anxious.

I accept that, while I might not be perfect, that's perfectly OK

Bearing all this in mind, please let it be known that I am also far from perfect. Despite mindfulness becoming a regular part of my life, and developing a bunch of tools to help me feel good, I'm still quite messy and unpredictable when it comes to my moods. I can still react rapidly to stress in a less-than-Zen way (instead of slowing down and responding wisely). I still often fall into piggy eating habits that are anything but mindful, turning to fatty and sugary foods in times of stress.

In fact—I'll be *really* honest here—I've had a very hard time writing this book. I got part way through it and had a huge emotional meltdown, got extremely stressed, cried a lot, sugar-binged like crazy and felt really miserable. The reason? I felt like a fraud writing a book about how to live well in sobriety when, in reality, I am still extremely messy and imperfect. How could I claim to have a template for successful sober living when I am still so flawed?

My first book, *Mrs D Is Going Without*, was easy to write because I was coming from a standpoint of strength and confidence. It was a doddle writing about the process of quitting alcohol when I was in such a robust position with my sobriety. I felt strong and clever—'Look at me, so happy to have turned my life around and be free of the booze!'—and I was extremely comfortable about sharing my story in the hope that it might help others.

But this book has been a different kettle of fish. This book isn't about a specific process, like how I stopped drinking; it has a much more general approach, as I've had to describe how I live now that I don't drink—and, on this front, (unlike the not-drinking) I feel far from confident or strong. In fact, I am so far from perfect it's not funny! How could I write some sort of self-help manual for living well when I don't always live well myself? I do not have all the answers.

I do not always make the best choices. I stumble and I fail. I am not a shining example of a perfect and clever self-help guru—far from it.

So, for quite a few weeks, writing this book was a hellish and emotional process. I got all stressed out, started waking up at 4 am, snapped more easily at the kids, ate loads of bad food, and sent myself all sorts of grumpy and hard-done-by mental messages (*Of course it's always me doing the dishes. Grumble, grumble...*). Whenever I talked to people about how the writing process was going, I cried. I cried all over my friends, sobbing, 'It's just so hard because I'm *so not sorted*.' I ate cake. I cried all over my mum and sister, saying tearfully, 'I'm just *not feeling strong* about what I've got to say.' I ate chips and dip. And I cried all over poor, long-suffering Corin, gulping, 'I'm *too unresolved* to do this.' I ate toast with butter and jam. He told me I could give up if I wanted. But I didn't.

A few things kept me going. One was my own stubbornness and determination. (Failure was not an option, and anyway I wanted to spend my advance on new blinds for the boys' bedrooms!) Another was the reaction I had from almost everyone I opened up to about my stress. 'No one is perfect, Lotta,' they said. 'You need to write about this struggle in the book,' they urged. 'Honesty is what people want,' they reassured. And remembering what the groovy summit expert Timothea Goddard said—that all of us are works in progress, not problems to be fixed or solved—helped me to relax about not being fully resolved or perfect.

And I also accepted that, in actual fact, despite still having a problem with sugar and still being messy and emotional and unresolved in many ways, I have progressed dramatically since I started my new project and I do have a bunch more tools at my disposal than I used to. While I'm very new to yoga and mindfulness and many of the concepts and habits I've written about in this book, being forced to review and explain them within these pages has helped enormously to cement them in my mind. I'm excited to forge ahead with putting them to good use—starting with practising compassion and forgiving myself for sugar-bingeing my way through the stress of writing this book. I'm also open to the contents of my toolbox shifting and changing as life goes on. Fluid all the way!

In actual fact, my toolbox has already changed a little since I wrote the first draft of this book. Stanley has ruptured his cruciate ligament and can't be walked for at least three months, which means we have lost our lovely daily jaunts up the hill. I really missed that regular exercise, so I've started going for walks with friends around the neighbourhood and have also—wait for it!—started doing yoga at home in the mornings. Can you believe it?! Maybe I will be sharing photos of myself doing handstands under waterfalls soon . . . Or maybe not. (Incidentally, Stanley's injury—just plain bad luck, apparently—has also been a real exercise in acceptance.)

If nothing else, I'm hoping that the readers of this book (hello, you!) will take away the idea that we all need a full toolbox to help us cope with life. We all need some go-to techniques that are nourishing, authentic, genuine and enriching. Tools that aren't about numbing and avoiding, but about being grounded, real and fully engaged in this crazy, messy ride called life.

Of course, other people's toolboxes will look vastly different to mine. Maybe running marathons is your go-to exercise, or a couple of cats have expanded the layers of love in your house. Maybe a Happiness Bowl is how you practise gratitude, or you meditate for twenty minutes every evening before bed. Maybe you dig bald Andy from Headspace or lotus-loving Deepak and Oprah. Maybe your connection to community comes from being a Scout leader or belonging to a netball team. Maybe gardening is how you nourish yourself, or not checking emails after 5 pm is how you stay in control of your internet usage.

I have friends who swear by hot yoga and do it three times a week! I've got friends who attend hour-long meditation classes every Monday, friends who frequent meditation websites I've never heard of, and friends who swear by mindfulness books I've never read. We are all so different, so of course our toolboxes are going to contain different things—and, what's more, there is such a vast array of fabulous material out there that we can't all possibly enjoy the same stuff. The one uniting factor is our need to have a range of habits, tools and techniques at our fingertips that inspire us, enrich us, strengthen us and relax us. Use the space on the next page to list your current tools and maybe some new ones you'd like to try. You can always cross things off again if they don't suit! What works for me isn't necessarily going to work for everyone.

I accept that, while I might not be perfect, that's perfectly OK. I accept that I am a normal woman with a messy range of human emotions, navigating as best I can this ever-changing, highly challenging experience called life. I'll forever be forgiving myself for my imperfections and moving forward, because treating myself with compassion is one of my biggest tools. I'm not boozing and numbing and avoiding; I'm facing every day in the raw, meeting every high and every low with a clear head and a brave, honest intention. And so long as I stay robust in my dialogue with myself and determined to continue to develop and grow as a sober woman, I'm OK with that.

I'm OK with that.

Resources

BOOKS

10% Happier: How I tamed the voice in my head, reduced stress without losing my edge, and found self-help that actually works—a true story
By Dan Harris
A very good read. He also has a website, app and podcast available here: 10percenthappier.com

A Mindfulness Guide for the Frazzled and *Sane New World: Taming the mind*
By Ruby Wax
I've read both of these books, and they are excellent.

Mindfulness: An eight-week plan for finding peace in a frantic world
By Mark Williams and Danny Penman
This is the brilliant book I followed to the letter. The accompanying audios are here: rodaledigitalbooks.com/mindfulness

Mrs D Is Going Without
By Lotta Dann
This is my first memoir, which tells the story of how I quit drinking.

Real Happiness: The power of meditation
By Sharon Salzberg
I love this woman! This book offers a 28-day programme to get you meditating. She also has loads of material and links available on her website: sharonsalzberg.com

The Happiness Trap: Stop struggling, start living
By Dr Russ Harris
I found this guy through the Mindfulness Summit and bought his book straight away. It offers fantastic, practical strategies for dealing with emotions.

The Mindfulness Revolution: Leading psychologists, scientists, artists, and meditation teachers on the power of mindfulness in daily life
Edited by Barry Boyce
A great collection of essays by leading experts in the field.

WEBSITES

Living Sober

livingsober.org.nz

This is the recovery website that I run. It provides a safe, free and anonymous online space for people to come together to talk about their relationship with alcohol. Our community is very kind, non-judgemental and powerful.

Mrs D Is Going Without

livingwithoutalcohol.blogspot.co.nz

This is my original blog, which I started just two days after I quit drinking. I still post here regularly.

The Mindfulness Summit

themindfulnesssummit.com

The entire Mindfulness Summit is still available here. You have to pay to access it now, but it is worth every penny!

Breathworks

breathworks-mindfulness.org.uk

This is a site for anyone dealing with pain, stress or illness. Vidyamala Burch is the co-founder of Breathworks and I heard her speak twice during the Mindfulness Summit.

Chopra Center Meditation

chopracentermeditation.com

This is Oprah and Deepak Chopra's site.

Doctor Albers

eatingmindfully.com

This is the site for Susan Albers, who is the mindful eating expert I heard about through the Mindfulness Summit.

Mindful

mindful.org

This is where I got the newsletter from that included '5 Tips for a Mindful Day'. Barry Boyce is editor-in-chief of this site.

Shamash Alinda

shamashalidina.com

Shamash is the fun and upbeat mindfulness expert I heard talk during the Mindfulness Summit. He wrote *Mindfulness for Dummies*.

Tara Brach

tarabrach.com

Tara is amazing and on her website makes freely available loads of guided meditations and hour-long talks.

Tiny Buddha

tinybuddha.com

This is the site run by Lori Deschene, who gave me my healthy internet tips. Her site is chock-full of enriching material.

APPS

Headspace

headspace.com

This might be your thing (it is for millions of people!).

Thank you

Thank you to the lovely team at Allen & Unwin—Jenny, Kimberley, Angela, Melanie and Becky.

Thank you to my test readers—Corin Dann, Alice Gilroy and Sue Kerr.

Thank you to Melli and Matt for putting on the amazing Mindfulness Summit and giving me permission to quote from it extensively.

Thank you to all the mindfulness experts of the world who share their wisdom and knowledge—often for free—through their books, websites and social-media pages.

Thank you to all my girlfriends, in particular my antenatal group (still going strong after twelve years!)—Robbie, Sarah C, Kath, Sarah G, Emma and Katy.

Thank you to all my extended family, particularly my parents, Chris and Tina, and my three sisters, Brita, Anna and Juliet.

Thank you to my fabulous sons, Axel, Kaspar and Jakob. And, Corin. Without you, nothing would be possible.

facebook.com/mrsdisgoingwithout
instagram.com/mrs_d_alcoholfree
twitter.com/mrsdalcoholfree

Want ideas for what to read next, competitions and news about your favourite authors?

Join us at:

Facebook
www.facebook.com/AllenAndUnwinNZ

Instagram
www.instagram.com/AllenAndUnwinNZ

Twitter
www.twitter.com/AllenAndUnwinNZ

ALLEN&UNWIN
www.allenandunwin.co.nz